IMMIGRATION
IMMIGRATION
IMMIGRATION
IMMIGRATION
QUESTIONS & ANSWERS

Carl R. Baldwin
ATTORNEY-AT-LAW

ALLWORTH PRESS, NEW YORK

For MaryEllen, Steve, and Kathleen

Published by Allworth Press, an imprint of Allworth Communications, Inc.
10 East 23rd Street, New York, NY 10010

Cover by Douglas Design Associates, New York, NY

Book design by Sharp Designs, Holt, MI

ISBN: 1-880559-32-3

Library of Congress Catalog Card Number: 95-76694

Contents

Preface

A chief purpose of this book is to help you avoid a costly immigration error.

This book is written for ordinary people who have an immigration question or problem, or who have a close relative or friend with an immigration question or problem. Every procedure that is described in the book would go more smoothly with the assistance of a good immigration lawyer. However, some readers will wish to go ahead and file their own petitions and applications. If so, the main purpose of the book is to give a step-by-step description of what you need to do in order to have a successful result. I intend to be clear and detailed enough to help you avoid an immigration misstep. These do occur when people take their immigration fate into their own hands.

Here's an example of the kind of error that this book will help you to avoid, based in part on a newspaper report about the Immigration and Naturalization Service (I have invented some details). A stepfather with a green card had filed a petition for his unmarried stepdaughter. It was approved by I.N.S., but, as we shall see, that approval was an error. Years later, the young woman was interviewed in her home country for an immigrant visa, with high hopes and the expectation that her visa would be issued routinely. But the consular officer discovered, and pointed out, that I.N.S. had made an error in approving the petition years ago: a petition by a stepparent is valid only if the marriage creating the relationship took place before the child turned eighteen. In this case, the child was eighteen when her mother married her stepfather. The whole procedure would have to be started from the beginning, with a petition by the mother. But there was a problem. Since the daughter had married in the meantime, the mother with a green card could not file a petition for her. The mother first had to become a naturalized U.S. citizen, a status that was years in the future. This is an example of what immigration heartbreak is made of, and this is the kind of misstep that this book will help you to avoid.

As we go along, we will suggest that there are certain kinds of procedures that you cannot handle on your own, and that require the help of a good immigration lawyer. The Appendix will give you some ideas on how to get competent legal assistance. You will also learn that the immigration law changes rapidly. Your lawyer, if you have one, will keep you up to date on changes in the law that apply to your situation. If you are undertaking a procedure on your own, we make some suggestions in the Appendix on how you can keep up to date with future changes by doing some homework. Use the information in this book as a solid foundation, which we believe to be accurate and reliable as we go to press. But make sure that you learn about any recent additions or alterations to that foundation before filing a petition or application to try to get yourself where you want to go.

I use a question and answer format to get as close as possible to a conversation with my readers, although I know that this imaginary conversation cannot amount to a legal consultation, since I cannot hear and answer the additional questions that will come up.

The book's emphasis, of course, in on the foreign citizen who has a question or problem. But I am also concerned about the U.S. employer who wants to stay on the right side of the immigration law, and I devote a chapter to giving that employer some guidance. And I devote another chapter to the legal resident or U.S. citizen worker who has been discriminated against by an employer because she looks or sounds "foreign."

The precious right that foreign citizens who fear persecution back home have to apply for political asylum is discussed, as well as the new rules that make getting work authorization more difficult for asylum applicants than it used to be. The procedure called adjustment of status is covered, with the new I.N.S. rules that may make it possible for you to stay in the U.S. and become a legal resident right here, rather than having to return home for a visa interview. I discuss the anti-immigrant mood that is now abroad in the land, and how this might affect legal as well as undocumented foreign citizens. Finally, I point to the goal that I hope many of my readers will have of becoming naturalized, and thus having all the rights and responsibilities of U.S. citizenship.

1

Is Immigration Good for the U.S.?

Today we are hearing voices questioning the long-held understanding that immigration, by reuniting families and bringing us some of the most talented people from around the world, has been, and still is, a great benefit to the United States of America. There are now writers and politicians who believe that immigration is "out of control," and that immigrants are taking jobs from American workers, and costing the U.S. taxpayer huge sums in public education, health care, and social services. This chapter will briefly look at some of the pros and cons about immigration.

---

1. *What is immigration?*
The word means "in-migration," to migrate in, to move in. It refers to the process by which foreign citizens,

technically known as "aliens," enter the U.S., legally or illegally, usually with the intention of taking up permanent residence here.

2. *Compared to what is going on throughout the world, how many refugees and asylum seekers are there in the U.S. at this time?*

The United Nations High Commissioner for Refugees (U.N.H.C.R.) estimates that, of the world's total refugee population, approximately 90% are in the developing countries, not in the so-called industrial democracies. The U.S. resettles a total of 120,000 refugees each year (refugees are screened at I.N.S. offices outside the U.S. for resettlement in the U.S.), and receives 150,000 asylum applications each year. It is estimated that less than 1.5% of the world's refugee population finds its way to the U.S. each year.

3. *How many so-called illegal immigrants are there, compared to legal immigrants?*

Let's start with definitions. A legal immigrant is a foreign citizen who enters the U.S. with a valid long term visa obtained from the U.S. Consulate in the home country. A so-called illegal immigrant is a foreign citizen who enters or tries to enter the U.S. without a visa from the U.S. Consulate in the home country, or someone who entered legally without needing a visa or with a valid short term visa, but then stayed longer than permitted by the Immigration and Naturalization Service (I.N.S.).

According to I.N.S., the U.S. each year settles 700,000 legal immigrants, 120,000 refugees, and 250,000 to 300,000 undocumented immigrants, for a total of 1.1 million. This means that about eight out of eleven immigrants enter the U.S. legally.

Of the 22 million foreign citizens in the U.S., I.N.S. estimates that 3.6 million are in undocumented status. Eighty-five percent (85%) of immigrants are here legally. Those who are here without proper papers are estimated to amount, in terms of numbers, to about 1.25% of the total U.S. population. Look around you from coast to coast, and about one out of a hundred people you see is an undocumented foreign citizen.

4. *How many undocumented immigrants entered legally in the first place?*

According to I.N.S., about half of the undocumented enter the U.S. by crossing the border with Mexico, and about half entered legally on short term visas, but then overstayed their permitted periods of stay. The three largest groups of overstays (as they are called) are Ecuadorians, Italians, and Poles. The overstays from Italy and Poland contradict the biased stereotype of the Mexican gatecrasher, and should remind us that stereotypes and bias are not helpful ways to think about immigration problems.

5. *What are the percentages and numbers for close relatives of U.S. citizens or legal residents, among the legal immigrants?*

Close family members get the lion's share of the total numbers: eighty percent (80%) of the total number of 700,000 each year go for family reunification (spouses, children, and parents of U.S. citizens; spouses and children of legal residents).

6. *Do immigrant workers have a bad effect on the U.S. economy?*

Not according to the U.S. Department of Labor. Their studies conclude that immigrants keep U.S. industries competitive, increase employment through higher rates of self-employment, and increase wages and mobility opportunities for many groups of U.S. workers.

7. *Do immigrants use a lot more in services than they pay in taxes?*

No. A study by the nonpartisan Urban Institute concluded that immigrants and refugees pay $28 billion a year more in taxes than they use in services. The study concludes that many are young, ambitious, entrepreneurial, and reluctant to use government services.

A federal study in 1992 found that undocumented foreign citizens made no attempt to use programs that they are, in any event, ineligible for: these included A.F.D.C. (Aid to Families with Dependent Children), Medicaid, and food stamps. State agencies that were required to monitor attempted use of services by the undocumented discovered a single attempt to get food stamp benefits in the entire country. The study concluded that the use of these services by the undocumented, contrary to expectations, was a non-issue.

8. *If this is so, why do some states complain about how much immigrants are costing them?*

The complaints and their causes are real enough. It does cost money to provide immigrants, including illegal immigrants, with a free public education through high school, which is required by a 1982 U.S. Supreme Court decision called *Plyler*. And a cause for complaint is that most of the taxes that immigrants pay go to the federal government, and do not get transferred back to the states. But this is really a problem of federal-state relations, not of immigration.

The undocumented population is concentrated in five states (in descending order): California, New York, Florida, Texas, and Illinois. Thirty other states have a total of less than 10,000 of the undocumented. A sensible approach to this imbalance has been suggested by the Director of the National Immigration Forum, a research organization: "The immediate solution is for the federal government to create a viable assistance program for areas that receive the majority of new arrivals—legal and not. Redistributing federal largesse that is now going to states without significant immigrant populations to those areas disproportionately impacted by new arrivals is an equitable and intelligent approach to deal with the real health, education and social service cost borne by state and local governments."

9. *Can undocumented foreign citizens walk in and get any kind of public service that U.S. citizens are eligible for?*

No. Under current law (and of course this may change to the disadvantage of the foreign citizen) they are only eligible for: emergency health care, schooling from kindergarten through high school, and the W.I.C. (Women, Infants, and Children) nutritional program.

10. *What is your answer to the question: is immigration good for the U.S.?*

It is unquestionably good for the U.S. Families have been reunited, and "family values" have thus been enhanced. People young and old have been able to realize the American dream by virtue of hard work and skill, which means not only making a living, but also living in a democracy and contributing to it. The United States has done itself proud, and has been an inspiration to other nations, by its policy of granting refugee status and asylum to those fleeing persecution under repressive and tyrannical regimes.

Foreign citizens who commit crimes continue to be a problem, but there are plenty of laws on the books to place them under proceedings, give them their day in court, and then, in many cases, require their return to their home countries.

The peace-loving and law-abiding immigrant, whether "legal" or "illegal," should not be treated with disdain, or scapegoated by writers, organizations, and politicians with an ax to grind.

11. *I read in a book that a change in the law back in 1965 led to an explosion of immigration, and that American society is now threatened by the results of that explosion. Is there anything to that?*

You are probably thinking of a recent book by Peter Brimelow called *Alien Nation*. Let's take a look at what the 1965 amendments to the law accomplished.

First, they established the system that is known as "family reunification" that will be an important part of this book (see chapters 8 and 12). In this system, U.S. citizens and legal residents can file petitions for very close relatives who are back home or in the U.S., and those relatives will be able to acquire legal residence in the United States. Important conservative politicians have praised "family values," and it certainly appears that the "family reunification" system is a fulfillment of that ideal.

Second, the 1965 amendments abolished the old system that gave preference to immigrants from European countries, the traditional source of immigration in the early twentieth century, and gave an equal opportunity to immigrate to citizens of any country around the world. From the point of view of the traditional American values of fairness and equality, it seemed like a good idea.

But Mr. Brimelow does not like it. He is nostalgic for the days when there was a very large majority of Americans who were white and English speaking. He is dismayed that the future may see a "browning" of America, as the descendants of dark-skinned people from Latin American, Africa, Asia, and India will become more noticeable on the American landscape.

One possible response to his concern about "browning" is: so what? So long as our new immigrants, and their children, obey our laws, pursue their education, and take care of themselves and their families, what on earth difference does the color of their skin make? One of my brown-skinned clients, a young man from Ethiopia, has just graduated from an American college with close to a perfect A average, and has won a prestigious medical research grant from the National Institute for Health. Can one imagine a more desirable immigrant?

You, the reader, can decide whether you think that Mr. Brimelow's approach is a sensible way to think about our immigration policies. In my opinion, it is based on stereotypes about "us" (immigrants and their descendants of European origin) and "them" (immigrants and their descendants from the rest of the world), and therefore cannot seriously contribute to a discussion of our immigration policies.

2

Green Card Defined

This chapter tells you what a so-called green card is, how long it lasts, and what to do to keep it valid. How to get it in the first place will take much of the book to describe.

---

1. *What is a green card?*

The term *green card* is a nickname for the plastic card that signifies that the holder is a lawful permanent resident of the United States (in this book we will generally use the shorter term *legal resident*). The plastic card was once green in color. It is now white, or pinkish, but the name green card is here to stay.

The official name for the card is Alien Registration Receipt Card. It is captioned Resident Alien at the top of the face of the card. The back of the card contains important identifying information. It is numbered I-551; an older version is numbered I-151.

2. *How long does a green card last?*

It used to last forever, or until the holder turned it in when becoming a naturalized citizen of the U.S.

Since September 1989, however, the green card has a life-span of just ten years (the expiration date is printed on the face of the card). Before this time is up, you must file an application to replace the card.

We think that it is a much better idea to become a naturalized citizen as soon as you are eligible to do so (usually either three or five years after getting the green card). This will bring important benefits and responsibilities, and also make it unnecessary to replace the card.

3. *But if I do not wish to become a U.S. citizen, and my ten year green card is about to expire, how do I keep it alive?*

You file the Form I-90 Application to Replace Alien Registration Card. Avoid a time consuming trip to the local office to pick up the form: obtain it by mail by phoning I.N.S. at 1-800-755-0777. You will make one trip to the local office to file the form and pay the fee of $75 to "Immigration and Naturalization Service" by check or money order. You include two identical color photographs, head and shoulders, looking to left, right ear visible. Write (do not sign) your name on the back of the photos with number 2 pencil, along with your A-number (the identifying number printed on the face of your green card). You complete two samples of the FD-258 Fingerprint chart, and write your A-number in the box noted as "Miscellaneous Number."

You enclose your ten-year card, and check box "f" under Part 2, paragraph 2, which says: "My present card has an expiration date on it and is expiring. I have attached my present card." Keep a photocopy of your card (both sides) for your records.

Do not change your address until you receive your replacement green card. But wouldn't you rather become a U.S. citizen? Think it over some more.

4. *What good is the green card to me?*

With the status that the card signifies, you can live permanently in the U.S., and work here at any job. You may be entitled to some public benefits, but watch out: the Congress that started work in January 1995 may reduce or eliminate some or many of those benefits.

You can travel outside the U.S. and use the card with your passport to reenter the country. If you have a criminal record, however, your green card will not guarantee that you can reenter the U.S. after a trip abroad. And the green card does not prevent you from being deported, if you commit a serious crime.

The date your green card was issued establishes a marker, and three or five years later you will be eligible to apply to be naturalized as a U.S. citizen.

5. *What are the different ways for me to get a green card?*

It will take most of this book to answer that question. As a starter, let's list the principal avenues that lead to legal residence and a green card:

- A petition filed by a U.S. citizen or legal resident for a close family member (see chapters 8 and 12);
- A petition filed for you by your employer, usually preceded by an application to the U.S. Department of Labor (see chapters 15 and 16);
- A successful application for political asylum, followed later by an application for what is called adjustment of status (see chapter 5);
- A successful application for the visa lottery (see chapter 7);

Cuban citizens who have entered the U.S. may adjust status to legal residence one year after entry (see chapter 18).

Once in a long while there is special legislation (like the so-called "amnesty" law of 1986) that leads to legal residence. But such legislation is extremely rare.

6. *How about giving me a list of which close relatives I can file a petition for to help them get a green card, and what my immigration status has to be in order to file that petition?*

If you are a legal resident (have a green card), you can file a petition for your spouse or unmarried child under age twenty-one (called Preference 2A), or your unmarried child age twenty-one or above (called Preference 2B). A green card holder cannot file a petition for a married child of any age, or for a parent.

If you are a U.S. citizen, you can file a petition for a spouse, unmarried child under age twenty-one, or parent (the citizen must be twenty-one or above to file for a parent.). These relatives are called immediate relatives. The citizen can also file for an unmarried child age twenty-one or above (called First Preference), a married child of any age (called Third Preference), and a brother or sister (called Fourth Preference).

Warning: The influential Commission on Immigration Reform urged in June, 1995 that the present Congress eliminate the First and Third Preferences, Preference 2B, and the Fourth Preference. This would have drastic consequences for many.

7. *Will the relatives called immediate relatives get their green cards faster than the others?*

Yes. If you are a U.S. citizen and petition for an immediate relative (spouse, unmarried child under age twenty-one, parent), they will get a green card more rapidly (or maybe I should say less slowly, because nothing happens overnight) than other relatives.

What is called an immigrant visa is immediately available to them, and they do not have to "wait in line," sometimes for years, as do some relatives who are in a less favored position.

8. *The green card is called the resident alien card. Who is an alien?*

The immigration law uses the term to mean anyone who is a foreign citizen and not a citizen of the United States. A resident alien is a legal resident of the U.S., but still an alien, and therefore subject to what is called exclusion (being kept out of the U.S. upon arriving or returning from abroad), and deportation (being sent back home once you are here). The only way to be immune from exclusion and deportation is to stop being an alien, and become a naturalized U.S. citizen.

In this book we will generally use the term foreign citizen rather than the technical term alien, which some foreign citizens find offensive.

9. *What does it mean to be an immigrant?*

If you are a foreign citizen, and if you have arrived at the port of entry or have entered the U.S. (legally or illegally) and intend to stay permanently, you are called an *immigrant*. To *immigrate* means to migrate in, to move in, and it brings with it the idea of moving in permanently.

10. *Isn't every foreign citizen in the U.S. an immigrant?*

Many are, but there is a different term, which is not in ordinary usage and you will not see it in the newspapers, that describes the foreign citizens who are not immigrants. The term is *nonimmigrant*. It's really not as peculiar as it looks at first. It just means any foreign citizen who is not an immigrant (who does not intend to stay in the U.S. permanently), and who has the kind of visa (called a nonimmigrant visa) that permits a legal, but temporary, stay in the U.S.

11. *What do I do if I lose my green card or if somebody steals it?*

You should start by reporting a theft of your card to your local police. To replace the card, you phone I.N.S. at 1-800-755-0777 and request Form I-90 Application to Replace Alien Registration Card. Follow the instructions, and file the form where indicated with check or money order for $75 made out to "Immigration and Naturalization Service." Refer back to Question 3 for more information about how to file for a replacement card. You check box "a" under Part 2, paragraph 1: "My card was lost, stolen, or destroyed. I have attached a copy of an identity document." At this point it would be ideal to enclose, as an identity document, a photocopy of both sides of the lost card, if you had made one: that would assist I.N.S. in making up the replacement card.

12. *Can my green card be taken away from me?*

Yes, if it is found that you provided false information to get the card, abandoned your U.S. residence, or committed a serious crime that subjects you to deportation. In that latter case you could lose the green card that you have, and never be able to get another one. Don't let this happen to you!

13. *The name on my green card is my married name. Can I change this name to my maiden name once I get my divorce?*

Yes. Once you have the divorce decree in hand, with its reference to your maiden name, use the Form I-90 with fee to I.N.S. of $75. You have to enclose the original of your green card, Form I-551. Make a photocopy of it (both sides) for your own records, and do not change your address until you receive the new card.

Check box "e" under Part 2, paragraph 1: "My name or other Biographic information has been changed since my card was issued. I have attached my present card and evidence of the new information" (this would be a copy of the divorce decree).

14. *I received my green card back in the 1970s, and it is not numbered I-551, but I-151. Is my old card still valid?*

It was scheduled to expire on March 20, 1995, but I.N.S. has extended the expiration date for one year until March 20, 1996.

After that date, you cannot use the old card to establish employment eligibility if you go looking for a new job, and, more important, you cannot use it to enter the U.S. legally after a trip abroad.

15. *Does that mean that my legal resident status will also expire?*

No. You will still be a legal resident. But you need to get the new Form I-551 card if you want to have the benefits that come with a valid, unexpired green card.

16. *When do I have to file to get the new green card?*

Do it right away. Do not wait until a few weeks before the deadline of March 20, 1996. You may find yourself without a card just when you need it.

17. *How do I do it?*

You file the Form I-90 Application to Replace Alien Registration Card (see Question 3, above, for basic information on filing this form). Phone the I.N.S. at 1-800-755-0777 to obtain the Form I-90. They will mail you the form, and you will have to make just one trip to the local office to file it.

18. *If I file for the new card, how long will it take for me to receive it?*

As we go to press, the waiting time is about six months.

19. *Can I get around this replacement problem by filing an application for naturalization now?*

Yes. If you file the N-400 Application for Naturalization before the expiration date of your old Form I-151 green card, you will not need to replace the old card and get the new Form I-551 green card. That would be a very good idea!

20. *Do I have to enclose my old expired card with my Form I-90 application?*

No. Unlike the situation with the new ten-year card, which you must enclose, you do not need to enclose the old Form I-151 with your application (just include photocopies of both sides of the card). Check box "j" under Part 2, paragraph 2, which says: "I have an old edition of the card."

21. *Let's pretend that I am reading this book from my home country, and it is after March 20, 1996. I forgot about the expiration of the old green card. A friend of mine mailed me the Form 1-90. Can I travel back to the U.S. and be allowed to enter?*

Fortunately, the answer is "Yes." Fill out the Form 1-90, and hand it to the immigration officer at the port of entry (with your $75 check and two photographs). You will not be turned back to the home country if you do this.

22. *Someone told me that I would lose my green card if I stayed outside the U.S. for more than a year. Is that true?*

Yes, it is. I.N.S. regulations make it clear that your green card will expire, and you will not be able to use it to reenter the U.S., if you remain abroad for more than one year.

23. *I have an urgent need to return home and take care of some business affairs. It's going to take me at least a year and a half to get everything done. Can I get special permission to depart and then return, without risking expiration of my green card?*

Yes, you can. You submit Form 1-131 Application for Travel Document, with the fee of $70 to the I.N.S.

24. *If I get the reentry permit, how long will it be good for?*

It will be valid for your reentry to the U.S. within two years after your departure.

25. *Can I file my application for the reentry permit once I arrive back home?*

No. The instructions to the form make it clear that you must be in the U.S. when you file your application.

26. *Can I ask I.N.S. to send me its notice of approval, if it is approved, to me in my home country?*

Yes. You can request that the notice of I.N.S. action be sent to you, care of the U.S. Consulate (or I.N.S. office) in your home country.

27. *I.N.S. approved me for a green card over six months ago at my adjustment of status interview. But I have not yet received my plastic card in the mail. What should I do?*

There is a form that will prompt I.N.S. to trace your green card, which was either slowed up in the manufacture, or was mailed out but never delivered or received. Use the Form G-731 Inquiry About Status of 1-551 Alien Registration Card (no fee) to prod I.N.S. to look into the explanation for this delay. If it is simply an overwork-related delay, this reminder should get things moving.

Obtaining a Short Term Visa

As a foreign citizen, you may get your first look at the United States as a result of obtaining a temporary stay visa (called non-immigrant visa), and then being admitted to the U.S. by an immigration officer for a temporary stay.

Once here, other things may happen. You may be able to get an extension of your stay, or change to a different temporary status. You may be able to change from temporary legal status to permanent legal status (get a green card), as a result either of marriage to a legal resident or U.S. citizen, or as a result of a job offer from a U.S. employer for a permanent position. In some cases, you may be able to remain in legal status as a result of making application for political asylum.

Depending on your country of citizenship, you may, in unusual cases, be eligible for Temporary Protected Status, permitting you to remain in the U.S. temporarily if your home country is ravaged by civil war or natural disaster.

And, of course, you may just stay for your allotted time, and then happily return to your home country.

This chapter will discuss the different kinds of temporary visas, and the challenge, once in the U.S., of maintaining your status or changing to one that you would rather have.

---

1. *I have a serious medical condition that doctors in my home country have been unable to diagnose. How can I get to the U.S. for medical treatment?*

You can get here in one of two ways. The first way is the Visa Waiver Pilot Program. Let's see what that is.

If you are a citizen of one of twenty-three countries (the list below is accurate as we go to press), you do not need a temporary stay visa (called nonimmigrant visa) from the U.S. Consulate in your home country. You just buy a round-trip ticket to the U.S. for a ninety day stay, and board the plane with your home country passport. The twenty-three countries are: Andorra, Austria, Belgium, Brunei, Denmark, Finland, France, Germany, Iceland, Ireland, Italy, Japan, Liechtenstein, Luxembourg, Monaco, Netherlands, New Zealand, Norway, San Marino, Spain, Sweden, Switzerland, and the United Kingdom.

Note: Ireland is designated on a probationary basis until September 30, 1998, at which time the designation will either be made permanent, or be terminated.

Comment on the Visa Waiver Program: it appears to be working well, and foreign citizens who used it in 1993 numbered in the millions. It is scheduled to end September 30, 1996. It is likely that the program will be continued: the short-term visitors have a good track record of going home within ninety days, and it is good for the U.S. economy (as well as for international relations) to have large numbers of foreign tourists who will speak well of the U.S.

The second way of getting here for medical treatment is to visit the U.S. Consulate in your home country and apply for the B-2 tourist visa (whether or not you are from a country that is eligible for the Visa Waiver program).

2. *Is there any disadvantage to the Visa Waiver Program?*

Yes. When you fill out a Form labeled I-94w, called Arrival and Departure Record, during your flight, you waive certain important rights. Here's what you agree to:

• Your stay is for a maximum of ninety days, and you cannot get an extension of stay; you cannot change to any other temporary stay status, such as the B-2 tourist status or F-1 student status;

- If the immigration officer at the port of entry decides that you cannot be admitted for any reason, you cannot challenge that decision before an immigration judge, and you can be returned home on the next flight;
- You cannot convert to legal resident status, unless you meet and marry a U.S. citizen during your ninety day stay or thereafter.

If that happens, the U.S. citizen could file a petition for you, and you could apply to adjust your status to legal resident (see chapter 8 for a description of how this works). If this happens, you could be "home free." Since you entered legally you will not be hit with the new $650 "penalty" fee (see chapter 8 for an explanation of this).

3. *I'm a citizen of Canada. Canada is not one of the countries eligible for the Visa Waiver Program. Does that mean that I need a visa to enter the U.S. from Canada?*

No. Canada is a special case. The U.S. and Canada have a cordial relationship, untroubled by the problem of illegal immigration from one country to the other. As a Canadian, you do not need a temporary stay visa to enter the U.S., unless you are coming to engage in international trade or investment, in which case you need to get an E-1 or E-2 visa (see discussion at Questions 81-88).

4. *But if I am a citizen of Mexico, I do need a visa?*

That's right. Immigration policy discriminates in favor of Canadians, and against Mexicans, when it comes to entering the U.S. without a visa. But Congress can do that: discriminating between foreign citizens with respect to entering the U.S. from abroad is perfectly legal.

5. *Wasn't N.A.F.T.A. (the North American Free Trade Agreement) supposed to help Mexicans, as well as Canadians, to enter the U.S.?*

Yes, but N.A.F.T.A. applies to a very limited population of Canadians and Mexicans : business people who would qualify as visitors for business (as in the B-1 visa, see Questions 57-61), or certain professionals. N.A.F.T.A. intends to enhance business and professional activities on both sides of the borders, but certainly does not intend to generally open the borders to free passage for our neighbors to the North and South.

6. *How do I get a B-2 tourist visa for a temporary stay in the U.S.?*

You visit the U.S. Consulate in your home country and fill out the Non-immigrant Visa Application. It is a U.S. Department of State Form that is labeled OF (Optional Form) 156 (it is not really optional—it is required for everyone who wishes to have any kind of temporary visa, including the tourist visa).

7. *Who looks at the application?*

It is reviewed, and approved or denied, by an officer of the State Department who is responsible for issuing visas. The officer is called a consular officer.

8. *What does the consular officer look for?*

Two things above all:

- The officer wants to be sure that you do not have what is called *immigrant intent* (have a hidden intention to stay permanently in the U.S., while telling the officer that you only plan a short visit);
- The officer wants to be sure that you are *admissible* to the U.S. (for example, that you do not have a criminal record, or a communicable disease of public health significance, either of which would exclude you from the U.S.).

9. *How do I prove that I do not have the intention of taking up long-term residence in the U.S.?*

In testing you out to see if you have the hidden intention to stay permanently, you will be asked if you have taken action, or if action has been taken on your behalf, that suggests that you are hoping and planning to reside long-term in the United States:

- Has a close relative filed a petition for you to help you get a permanent stay (immigrant) visa?
- Has an employer filed a labor certification application for you (a first step toward an immigrant visa)?
- Have you expressed a wish to a consular officer to reside permanently in the U.S.?

If you answer "Yes" to any of these questions, the consular officer will be justified in finding that you have immigrant intent (the intention to stay permanently), and will not issue a temporary stay (nonimmigrant) visa.

Here's the general rule: if you have a so-called dual intent, the wish to get a temporary stay visa for now but the ultimate goal of obtaining permanent legal residence in the U.S., you will be denied the temporary stay (nonimmigrant) visa.

Here's the exception to the general rule: if you are making application for the H-1B visa as a worker in what is called a specialty occupation (see below, Questions 64-66), you may be able to get the visa even if a close relative or employer has already filed a petition that is intended to lead you to permanent residence. In that case, a dual intent is allowed: your ultimate goal, to get a green card, does not cancel out your immediate goal of getting a temporary work visa and entering the U.S. in that status.

Some of you may be able to take advantage of this exception to the general rule.

10. *Do I need to show the consular officer documents to prove that I do not intend to remain permanently in the U.S.?*

There are a number of things that you have to prove, and documents will help. You need to show that you have a foreign residence that you have no intention of abandoning. Documents to prove this could include an apartment lease or proof of home ownership, a letter from an employer stating that he or she is expecting you back by a certain date, or proof that you are a full-time student and that classes will resume on a certain date.

You also need to show that you have the financial resources to support yourself during your temporary stay in the U.S. If you will be staying with a relative who will provide for you, get a notarized letter or Form I-134 Affidavit of Support from that relative so stating, and describing his or her ability to put you up for that period of time.

11. *If I am going for medical care, do I need a letter from my home country doctor?*

You should get a letter from your home country doctor, stating why local resources are not adequate to handle your case, and naming the U.S. medical center that the local doctor recommends for your diagnosis and treatment.

12. *If I get a visitor's visa, what activities am I permitted to engage in while in the United States?*

You are permitted to visit, to tour, to recreate, to see the sights, to enjoy the arts, theater, music, and films. You can attend forums and symposiums. You may participate in them, so long as you do not receive any payment for your participation. You can, of course, if this is what you are coming for, receive medical diagnosis and treatment.

13. *What am I not allowed to do with a B-2 visitor's visa?*

You are not allowed to engage in a full course of studies at any educational institution, and you are not allowed to be gainfully employed.

14. *What does a temporary stay (nonimmigrant) visa look like?*

It is not a separate piece of paper, like the 8½ by 11 inch page that is the permanent stay (immigrant) visa. It is, instead, a stamp that is placed in your home country passport, and that fills up an entire passport page.

15. *Does my temporary stay visa guarantee that I will be able to enter the U.S.?*

No. The only thing that the temporary stay visa guarantees is that you will be able to board the airplane in your home country and get as far as the international airport in the U.S. where your plane touches down, which is called the port of entry.

16. *What if my visa is valid indefinitely, and is for an unlimited number of entries. Doesn't that mean that I can enter and reenter the U.S. as often as I like?*

No, it does not mean that. And a number of people have been very unpleasantly surprised to be carrying that kind of visa, and yet to be stopped at the gate and not permitted to enter the U.S.

The visa that you have, like any other temporary stay visa, means that you can travel to the port of entry in the U.S. and be inspected there by the immigration officer. An indefinite validity and unlimited entry visa does not mean that you have any right to be admitted to the United States.

17. *What happens at the port of entry?*

If you are admitted, and not turned away, the immigration officer who admits you will stamp your passport with the date of admission and the location of the port of entry. The officer will then stamp the I-94 Arrival and Departure Record that you filled out on the plane with the same information, and will write by hand your B-2 visa category, and your period of authorized stay. The Departure Record part of the I-94 is stapled to one of the passport pages.

18. *If I am admitted by the immigration officer, how long will I be allowed to stay?*

You will be admitted for six months. If you have a very good reason to ask for an extension of stay, you may be given an additional six months, for a total of one year.

19. *What happens if the I-94 comes loose from the staple, and I lose it?*

You will need a replacement in order to prove your duration of stay, to apply for an extension of stay or change of status, and to prove that you are eligible to adjust status to legal resident without paying the $650 "penalty" that is imposed on adjustment applicants who did not enter the U.S. with a valid nonimmigrant visa.

To replace the lost I-94, you fill out Form I-102, Application for Replacement of Initial Nonimmigrant Arrival/Departure Record, with payment to I.N.S. of $65. I.N.S. is supposed to keep a record of each foreign citizen who is admitted to the U.S. for a temporary stay, and should be able to replace the I-94 with the relevant information about visa category and period of authorized stay.

Here's a common sense suggestion: as soon as you get the I-94, make a photocopy of it. That copy will greatly facilitate its replacement, and may even be enough to prove that you were inspected and admitted when it becomes necessary to prove that fact.

20. *What happens to me if I get a job?*

You are in B-2 tourist status, which prohibits employment. If you go to work, you violate your status. If I.N.S. finds out about the violation of status, you could be placed under deportation proceedings and forced to return to your home country. If you are deported, you will be unable to be readmitted to the U.S. for five years.

21. *If I.N.S. discovers that I am working, is that something that can hurt me in the future?*

Yes. The I.N.S. and the Department of State may exchange information about foreign citizens. If you return to your home country and try to get another temporary stay visa, the fact that you violated status on your first visit (if the consular officer knows about it) could prevent you from getting another visa.

22. *If I start working right away, is that a bigger problem?*

Yes. If you start working within thirty days of admission with a B-2 visa, it is more serious. The State Department and I.N.S. will conclude that you lied to the consular officer when you applied for the B-2 visa, and assured the officer that you understood that you were prohibited from working. That lie can haunt you for the rest of your career as a foreign citizen trying to get into the U.S.

A lie to a consular officer is called *misrepresentation,* and can prevent you from ever again getting any kind of visa, or being admitted to the U.S. (if the State Department and I.N.S. know about it). Suggestion: think very seriously before violating your B-2 status by working as soon as you are admitted to the U.S..

23. *What happens if I discover that my medical treatment is going to take longer than my permitted period of stay?*

You should apply for an extension of stay, and will probably get it for a valid medical reason. You use Form I-539 Application to Extend/Change Nonimmigrant Status, with payment of $75 to "Immigration and Naturalization Service."

24. *Is there a problem if I wait until the last minute to apply for an extension of stay?*

There could be a problem if you try to rush I.N.S. to make a last minute decision. Instructions to the Form I-539 advise that you file for extension as soon as you learn that it will be necessary, and, in any event, not less than forty-five days before the date of expiration of your six month permitted stay.

25. *I did not learn from my doctor that additional treatment would be required until the week before my period of stay expired. I was just too worried after that, and did not think of applying for an extension. Am I out of luck?*

Maybe not. Instructions to Form I-539 state that a failure to meet the deadline may be excused if:
- The delay was due to extraordinary circumstances beyond your control; the length of the delay was reasonable;
- You have not otherwise violated your status (for example, by working or undertaking full-time studies);
- You are still a bona fide nonimmigrant (you have not taken action that could lead to permanent legal status);

- You are not in deportation proceedings (I.N.S. is not trying to send you back to your home country).

You should get a notarized letter from your doctor stating that you were informed only recently of the need for further treatment. This will prove that circumstances beyond your control contributed to the delay. And the length of the delay, from what we can see here, was reasonable.

26. *What documents do I submit with my application for an extension of stay?*

You must submit the original of your Form I-94 Departure Record (make a photocopy to keep for yourself). The back of the Departure Record, under Record of Changes, is where I.N.S. notes the date of its approval of the application for extension of stay, and the date to which your stay is extended.

27. *Where do I file my application for extension?*

Check the instructions to Form I-539 for this. For a B-2, file at your local I.N.S. office.

28. *How do I learn whether my application is approved?*

If it is approved, you will get back a notice of approval, and the original I-94 Departure Record, with the approval date and the date of extension written on the back.

29. *What do I do if it is not approved?*

Nothing. Or, I should say, nothing about the denial, since there is no right to appeal a denial of the application for extension.

Other actions may be possible for you, especially if you meet and marry a legal resident or U.S. citizen. See chapter 8 for a discussion of these possibilities.

30. *After being admitted in B-2 status, I learned about a college near where I am staying that has a program of studies that I would love to get into. Can I change from B-2 status to student status?*

It is possible, but difficult, to change from visitor status to student status.

Let's give a little background on the whole question of changing from one temporary stay status (nonimmigrant status) to another.

There are some persons in temporary (nonimmigrant) status who cannot change to another temporary status. They are persons who entered:

- In the Visa Waiver Pilot Program (see above, Questions 1-2);
- With a transit visa (C visa);
- As transits without visa;
- As crewmen on a ship or plane (D visa);
- As exchange students or scholars (see below, Questions 37-43 for a discussion of the J-1 visa and its severe limitation on change of status).

There is no bar to a B-2 changing to a full-time student, which is the F-1 status, but I.N.S. will want to know why you didn't get the F-1 visa in the first place, if you intended to be a student in the U.S. You have to explain, in a notarized statement that you include with your change of status application (Form I-539), that you fully intended to come as a visitor and then return home, but that unexpected events have turned you toward the idea of changing status to full-time student. For example, you might have run into an acquaintance who told you about the college, and caused you to become enthusiastic and think that this was exactly what you would like and need. Remember, you must at all costs avoid the suspicion that you lied to the consular officer and the immigration officer when you got your B-2 visa and entered the U.S., and were all the time cooking up a plan to change to student status.

You must also convince the I.N.S. that, up until now, you have been in proper B-2 status: no full-time study, and no gainful employment. If you have already violated your B-2 status, you will not be permitted to change to a different nonimmigrant status.

31. *What documents do I need to back up my application to change to student status?*

The same documents that you would have needed if you had gone to the U.S. Consulate in your home country to apply for an F-1 visa. These are:

Form I-20 A-B (school copy)/I-20 I.D. (student copy) Certificate of Eligibility for Nonimmigrant Student Status. This is the form that you will receive from the school that has accepted you as a full-time student.

Your passport must have a validity date that extends at least six months beyond the expected date of termination of your full course of studies.

You must also submit the original of your Form I-94 Departure Record, together with the Form I-539 Application to Extend/Change Nonimmigrant Status, with fee of $75 to "Immigration and Naturalization Service."

You need to prove that you have the financial resources to live as a full-time student, at least for your first two semesters.

32. *Where do I file to change from B-2 to F-1?*

The instructions to Form I-539 give you the answer. For a change from B-2 to F-1, you file at your local I.N.S. office.

33. *How do I learn whether my application is approved?*

You will get a written notice of approval, and the return of your I-94 Departure Record indicating the change to F-1 student status, and its period of validity (it will be for "duration of status," as long as your full-time student status continues).

34. *If I succeed in changing to F-1 status, am I entitled to work in that status?*

Yes, but to a very limited degree.

As soon as you enroll as a full-time student (defined as twelve credit hours, normally four courses of three credit hours each) you may work on campus, typically in the student cafeteria or bookstore, for up to twenty hours per week during the semester when school is in session. During holidays and vacations, you can work on campus full-time.

If you work outside of these narrow limits, you are in violation of status, and for that reason, if I.N.S. finds out about it, you are subject to deportation.

35. *Do I have to maintain full-time studies in order to be in status?*

Yes. The only exception to this rule would be if you had a serious medical problem that prevented you from carrying on full-time studies during a particular semester. In that case, the rule would be suspended for a semester.

36. *Am I permitted to work off-campus?*

Yes, to a limited degree, but your employer must follow strict rules to enable you to qualify. Keep in mind, first of all, that the program providing for off-campus work for F-1 students is not long term: it expires September 30, 1997.

While it lasts, it limits you to twenty hours per week of off-campus work, whether school is in session or on vacation. Your prospective employer must go to the trouble of filing what is called an Attestation (statement under oath) with the U.S. Department of Labor, stating that the employer has tried for sixty days to recruit a U.S. worker for your position, without success. This Attestation must also be filed with the official on campus in charge of foreign student affairs, called the Designated School Official (D.S.O.) by I.N.S. Your employer states that you will be paid wages appropriate for the job (not paid a low wage in order to undercut U.S. workers), and that your employment will be limited to twenty hours per week.

37. *I entered the U.S. in J-1 status as an exchange scholar, and my studies are financed by the government of my home country. I have married a U.S. citizen, and would like to adjust status to become a legal resident. Is there any problem with that?*

Yes. There may be a big problem with that.

Here's where you need a good immigration lawyer. Your lawyer first needs to find out whether your J-1 status is subject to something called the two year foreign residence requirement. If it is not, you are home free, and can go ahead and adjust status (see chapter 8 on how to do it).

But if your studies are funded by the home country (or the U.S. government), you are subject to the requirement, and that's where your troubles begin. Even though married to a U.S. citizen, which is normally the "fast track" to adjustment to legal residence, you cannot adjust, until you return home for two years, or obtain a waiver of that requirement.

38. *Can I satisfy the foreign residence requirement by going back home, but making trips to the U.S. to see my wife and check in with my professors and advisors?*

No. The law says that the J-1 cannot change status to legal resident until they have first returned to the home country for two years of what is called *physical presence*. That term means that you have to be there every day of the week for two years, except for very brief departures from the home country that do not disturb the uninterrupted physical presence there. In other words, you cannot reside in the home country but make long trips to the U.S. to visit your spouse and pursue your studies. You must remain in the home country for two unbroken years.

39. *Isn't there a loophole to get around this harsh law?*

Yes, there is a possible loophole (called a waiver), but it is not an easy one to find. You have to return home for two years unless you can prove either that your U.S. citizen or legal resident spouse (and child, if any) would suffer exceptional hardship (either if they went to your home country with you, or if you went there on your own and left them in the U.S.), or that you yourself would be persecuted in your own country on the basis of race, religion, or political opinion.

40. *What is the form to file and the fee to pay to apply for this waiver?*

You file the Form I-612 Application for Waiver of the Foreign Residence Requirement, and pay the fee to I.N.S. of $95.

41. *How does my lawyer show that I would be persecuted in my home country?*

Your lawyer practically has to show that your name is on a hit list that has been read on the government radio by the dictator of your home country. It's almost that bad. This is because the statute that describes the waiver of the two year foreign residence requirement states that you must prove that you "would be persecuted." In other words, that it is not just possible, but probable, that your government would hunt you down as soon as it learns that you have returned home.

This standard is much tougher than the usual asylum standard that we will look at in chapter 5, where you have to show that you have a "well-founded fear" of persecution in your home country: not a probability, but just a reasonable possibility of persecution.

With this tough standard, immigration lawyers generally feel that it is not possible to win a waiver of the foreign residence requirement on the basis of persecution.

42. *Well then, how does my lawyer show that my spouse would be subject to exceptional hardship if I have to fulfill the two-year foreign residence requirement?*

Let's think about that. Remember, you have to show exceptional hardship to your spouse in either of these two situations:
- If she returns with you to your home country for two years of physical presence there; or
- If you return on your own, leaving her in the U.S. without you.

Keep in mind that the term exceptional hardship means that you must show far more than just the usual or expected hardship that will occur if you leave your U.S. citizen spouse or if the two of you return to your home country. A mere come-down in the standard of living from the U.S. to the home country, in other words, will not suffice to show exceptional hardship.

Do you and your spouse have certain sensitivities or vulnerabilities that would spell out an intolerable situation, either for you to be separated from one another, or for the two of you to have to return to your home country? Are there medical problems and difficulties, including psychological and emotional factors, that would mean that either a separation or a return to your home country would be insufferable, and be an exceptional hardship? You should, if this is pertinent, confer with doctors and psychologists or psychiatrists to see how severe a hardship this might be.

If the two of you have a child born in the U.S., and therefore a U.S. citizen, any severe detriment to that child as a result either of separation from you, or as a result of returning with you to your home country and thereby being cut off from his or her own country and culture, should be emphasized. Either separation from a parent at a tender age, or the dislocation of being taken to a foreign country and culture, could be traumatic, and could constitute exceptional hardship.

Exceptional hardship to your spouse or child, rather than your probable perse-cution, is the best path to follow. But know that it is not at all easy to get this waiver.

43. *Can my U.S. citizen spouse get her Congressional representative to sponsor a private bill to waive the requirement that I return to my home country for two years?*

No. The J-1 visa was thought out by Congress as an instrument of foreign relations. Students would get the benefit of training in the U.S. at government expense, but promise to return to their home country to be of service there. The only time that Congress passed a private bill to waive the J-1 foreign residence requirement was in 1955, and it was vetoed by the President for foreign policy reasons. At present both the House and Senate rules on private bills preclude consideration of a private bill to waive the J-1 foreign residence requirement.

44. *I have some different questions about the J visa. If I enter the U.S. in J-1 status with my spouse in J-2 status, can either of us work for a living in the U.S.?*

The answer is "No," but with an explanation. You, as the J-1, cannot get a job. The theory is, and we hope it is also a reality, that your home country funding will enable you to live adequately in the U.S.

Your spouse is entitled to work, but the law states that she is to earn income to enhance her recreational or cultural activities (going to plays and concerts, for example), not for the purpose of supporting the family, which your funding is supposed to do.

45. *How does my wife get permission to work in the U.S.?*

She writes (c)(5) (spouse or child of exchange visitor) at box 16 of the Form I-

765 Application for Employment Authorization, and encloses a copy of the J-1 Certificate of Eligibility (form IAP-66) with $70 fee.

New I.N.S. rules require that the application, with photos and fingerprints, be mailed to the Service Center specified in the instructions. The Employment Authorization Document (E.A.D.) will be picked up at the local office or mailed to your wife, and will be valid for four years.

46. *I have a young friend who has an invitation from an American family to spend the summer months with them, taking care of the kids and doing some chores around the house. Is there a visa that he could apply for?*

Believe it or not, the J-1 visa is right for him, even though he is not a typical exchange student or scholar. Here's how the U.S.I.A. (United States Information Agency) explained the purpose of the au pair program: "The au pair program is an exchange program designed to provide foreign youth from less affluent backgrounds between ages eighteen and twenty-five the opportunity to visit the United States so that they can learn about American culture, improve English language skills, and assist American host families with child care while living with them as guest members. The idea is to create a cross-culture exchange through the interaction of au pairs and the family members."

47. *How does my friend get this visa?*

The American family needs to contact the U.S. agencies that have taken the responsibility for overseeing the au pair program. They are: Experiment in International Living, tel. (202) 371-9410; American Institute for Foreign Study, tel. (203) 869-9090; EF Au Pair, tel. (617) 225-3838. These agencies will explain what has to be done to get your friend the visa.

48. *What does the American family have to do, and what does my young friend have to do?*

The family has to provide a home for your friend, and treat him like a family member, not like a servant. The family pays your friend about $125 per week and provides room and board.

49. *Does my friend have to take courses?*

Yes. He should attend classes and attend cultural events (this part should be fun) for at least two evenings per week.

50. *Can the host family work my friend around the clock?*

No. Your friend is committed to do child care and light house work for 5½ nine-hour days per week. No extremely heavy work should be assigned.

51. *Does my friend have to put money down as security?*

Yes. He puts $500 in escrow, and it is returned when he departs from the U.S.

52. *What's in it for the organization that was helpful in arranging the program with the American family and my friend?*

In addition to the satisfaction of being helpful to international relations, it gets $50 per week for arranging the program and monitoring it so that both the American family and the au pair play by the rules.

53. *How long can my friend remain in the program?*

It can last as long as one year, but as a practical matter it is usually a summer program.

54. *Will the J-1 au pair program continue indefinitely?*

No. The U.S.I.A. has lost enthusiasm for it, and it is likely to be phased out by the end of the 1990s.

55. *I am a citizen of the People's Republic of China, and came here in J-1 status. Someone told me that the foreign residence requirement does not apply to Chinese students. Is that true?*

It was true for a while, but is no longer.

It was true under a law called the Chinese Student Protection Act (C.S.P.A.), enacted October 9, 1992. Chinese students who had been in the U.S. by June 5, 1989 (the date of the Tiananmen Square massacre), and before April 11, 1990, were permitted to apply for adjustment to legal residence, and the two year foreign residence requirement of the J-1 visa was waived.

But the application period ended June 20,1994. If you did not apply for adjustment by that date, the waiver of the residence requirement does not apply to you.

56. *Does this mean that I have to go back to China?*

Hold on. You can still apply for a waiver of the foreign residence requirement. It just means that the automatic waiver of the C.S.P.A. no longer applies to you.

57. *I am a business person. What is the right visa for me?*

There is a visa that is called the B-1 visitor for business visa. Its purpose is to further international trade and commerce. For that reason, it is not a free ride to come to the U.S. and shop around for employment. You cannot be paid by a U.S. source for working here. Instead, you must be paid by your home country employer for the work that you do here for that employer.

58. *As a business visitor, do I qualify for the same Visa Waiver program that the tourist does?*

Yes, if you are a citizen of one of the eligible countries (see above, Question 1).

59. *What are some examples of what the B-1 business visitor can do here?*

A good example is the clothier who takes measurements of American customers for clothes manufactured abroad. Payment is made to the foreign company and the clothes are delivered to the U.S. customers. The example would serve equally well for any article made abroad and purchased by the American customer, as a result of the salesmanship of the B-1 visitor for business.

60. *I am a sculptor. Can I get a B-1 visa to try to interest U.S. customers in my work, and maybe drum up some commissions for new work from people who see my work in my studio and like it?*

Probably not. I.N.S. would look at your proposal as a plan to drum up business and trade for yourself, not a plan that will have a positive impact on international trade and commerce.

61. *I make quite a few trips to the U.S. to conduct business for my home country employer. Can't I.N.S. do something to make my arrivals easier and less time consuming?*

I.N.S. has adopted a fast-track program for business people like you called INSPASS. At the moment, it is in operation at the airports at New York and Newark, New Jersey. You provide data, I.N.S. puts it onto a wallet sized card, and with that card you can enter the U.S. at least three times a year without having to undergo the usual inspection by the immigration officer. Just show the card and enter the U.S. without further delay.

If you are entering from Toronto, Canada, you can get your INSPASS card processed there as well.

62. *I am about to graduate from a four year college with a major in computer science. I have a job offer from the city for a computer programmer. What can I do to be able to take that job?*

You need to change status from F-1 (full-time student) to the status called H-1B.

63. *Can I do that on my own?*

No. Unlike the change from B-2 (tourist) to F-1 (full-time student), which you can try on your own, a change to H-1B status must be asked for by your prospective employer. That employer, in turn, will need to work with a good immigration lawyer, not with you.

However, while you are getting that lawyer (the employer, if it does this a lot, may already have one), let's give an overview of what the H-1B status is, and how you may qualify for it.

64. *What is H-1B status?*

Since the Immigration Act of 1990, the definition of H-1B has been: member of a *specialty occupation.*

You have to qualify for the so-called specialty occupation, and your employer has to need you to work in that occupation.

65. *How do I qualify to be in a specialty occupation?*

You qualify if your occupation requires the theoretical and practical application of a body of highly specialized knowledge, and attainment of a bachelor's or higher degree in that specialty.

Your four-year college degree (that's the basic bachelor's degree) will be your ticket to a specialty occupation.

66. *Which fields of study qualify for the H-1B?*

The immigration law does not give a list from A to Z, but does give some examples. The examples given (and they are just an illustration, they do not exhaust the allowable fields of endeavor) are: architecture, engineering, mathematics, physical sciences, social sciences, medicine and health, education, business specialties, accounting, law, theology, and the arts.

It looks as if computer science would fit under the heading of a business specialty.

67. *I am a performing artist, still in the home country. Is the H-1B the right visa for me?*

No. If you are a performing artist, you will need to look to one of the two new visas that came in with the Immigration Act of 1990: either the O-1 or the P-1 visa (we will discuss them later).

68. *Getting back to me, the F-1 student wishing to change to H-1B. What does my prospective employer have to do?*

Your employer does two things: requests a change of status for you by filing the Form I-129 Petition for a Nonimmigrant Worker, with payment of $75 to "Immigration and Naturalization Service," and files with the U.S. Department of Labor ETA Form 9035 Labor Condition Application for H-1B Nonimmigrants.

69. *What does my employer state in the Form I-129?*

The employer checks box 2(a) to show that this is new employment, and checks box 4(b) to request that your status be changed from what is it is now to H-1B. Your employer will have to include a certified copy of your diploma, showing that you got the bachelors' degree, and should include a certified copy of your official transcript, showing that your field of concentration was computer science.

Your employer confirms that the job that is offered requires the skill level of an employee who has specialized knowledge and the bachelor's degree. The employer must also state that it is the custom in the business to employ a person with the bachelor's degree to do this kind of work.

70. *What does my employer put into the Labor Condition Application?*

Your employer must make an attestation (sworn statement) in the application that the wages paid to you will be at least the actual wage level for the occupational classification at the place of employment, or the prevailing wage level for the occupational classification in the area of employment, whichever is greater.

Your employer must also state that the working conditions for you will not adversely affect the working conditions of U.S. workers.

71. *Let's say that I.N.S. approves my employer's petition to change my status. How long can I stay in* H-1B *status?*

Your initial period of stay is for three years. You may apply for extensions of stay of up to a total of six years.

Keep in mind, however, that the Labor Condition Application, once approved by the Department of Labor, is only valid for three years.

72. *If I get a better job as a computer programmer, can I take my* H-1B *status with me to my second job?*

No. Your H-1B status is employer-specific. If you want to change jobs, your new employer has to start from scratch and file the Form I-129 petition for you.

73. *If I return home for a vacation, what is the visa that I show when I reenter the U.S.?*

Your question shows us the difference between having a visa, and having a status.

Your status is now H-1B, since your employer helped you to obtain a change from F-1 to H-1B. But the visa in your foreign passport still says F-1. With your change of status, it is no longer of any use to you.

When you get to your home country, you will have to spend some time at the nonimmigrant (temporary stay) section of the U.S. Consulate, show the evidence of your change of status, and get a new visa stamp in your passport. With that new H-1B visa stamp in your passport, you can reenter the U.S.

74. *I am a fashion model, still back in the home country. I have a job offer from a high level modeling agency in the U.S. I do not have a bachelor's degree in a specialty occupation. What is the right visa for me?*

Believe it or not, there is a place for you as an H-1B visa applicant. I guess this shows that the fashion industry does effective lobbying, because otherwise your profession does not exactly fit. Your employer does the usual thing: files the Form I-129 petition, and the Labor Condition Application. The employer has to prove that you are a model of what is called distinguished merit and ability, which means a very, very high level of ability, with an employment record, photos, and publicity to prove it.

Since you are still in the home country, your prospective employer in the U.S.

files the Form I-129 with I.N.S. Once approved, it is sent to the U.S. Consulate in your home country for issuance of the visa.

75. *I have been trained as a nurse in my home country. Is the H-1B visa the right one for me?*

No. There is another visa that is right for you: it is called the H-1A, and it is just for nurses. I will give you a brief sketch of it, but you will need a lawyer, and your employer (which is probably a hospital) to help you through all of the hurdles to getting this visa. It is not something that you can do on your own.

76. *How do I qualify for the H-1A visa?*

You must intend to come to the U.S. temporarily to work as a nurse, and meet certain specific requirements.

77. *What are those requirements?*

You have to show:

- That you have obtained a full and unrestricted license to practice professional nursing in your home country, or were educated in the U.S. or Canada;
- That you passed the exam in the U.S. that is specified in regulations published by the U.S. Department of Health and Human Services.

You can omit the above two requirements if you have a full and unrestricted license to practice professional nursing under state law in your state of intended employment.

78. *What does my employer, a hospital, have to prove to I.N.S.?*

That the U.S. Department of Labor has what is called an attestation on file from the hospital, and that it is unexpired. In the attestation the hospital says that there would be a substantial disruption in services, through no fault of its own, if it could not employ you (and other foreign citizen nurses) to deliver health care services.

The hospital also states that your employment will not have an adverse effect on the wages and working conditions of others similarly employed (of U.S. workers).

The hospital states, finally, that it is making every effort to recruit and retain U.S. citizen or lawful immigrant nurses, so that it will eventually not be dependent on foreign citizen nonimmigrant nurses.

In the meantime, as the reader will know if he or she has been a patient or just a visitor lately in an American hospital, foreign citizen nurses are doing a magnificent job of caring for us and our loved ones.

As with the Form I-129 petition for H-1B that is filed for the foreign citizen who is still abroad, I.N.S. decides the petition, and, if it is approved, forwards it to the U.S. Consulate in the home country for issuance of the visa.

79. *I am a sugar-cane cutter from Jamaica. Is there a visa that will get me to the U.S. to do this kind of work?*

Yes, there is. It is the H-2A visa, for temporary agricultural work. The employer files the Form I-129 petition after obtaining from the U.S. Department of Labor a temporary labor certification for an agricultural worker, that will cover you and many workers like you. If it is approved, it is forwarded to the U.S. Consulate in the home country for issuance of the visa.

In an effort to safeguard the interests of American workers, the U.S. Department of Labor requires that employers hire any qualified U.S. worker who applies for the job until 50% of the work contract has been completed. Even with this open door safeguard for American workers, studies suggest that as few as 3% are interested in undertaking this backbreaking labor. We can draw this conclusion: U.S. sugar cane would not get cut, and U.S. crops would not get harvested, but for the efforts of foreign citizen workers.

80. *What are the different jobs that H-2A workers do, and where do they do them?*

In 1992, the most recent year in which the question was studied, it worked out like this: 30% of the workers were apple pickers, and worked in the Northeast and Middle Atlantic states; 27% were tobacco harvesters in Southern states; 22% were Jamaican sugar cane cutters in Florida; 8.5% were sheepherders (this trade is under H-2A, although not exactly agricultural work).

81. *I have made a lot of money in my home country, and I would like to come to the U.S. to start a business. Is there a visa for me for that purpose?*

If there is a treaty of trade and commerce between the U.S. and your home country, there may well be a visa for you.

The E-1 visa is for a treaty trader; the E-2 is for a treaty investor. Let's start with the investor.

82. *How do I qualify for a treaty investor E-2 visa?*

You must intend to enter the U.S. solely for the purpose of directing the operations of an enterprise in which you have invested, or are actively in the process of investing, a substantial amount of capital.

83. *What is meant by a substantial amount of capital?*

There is not a dollar figure that goes with the term substantial. What is substantial for you is measured against your overall resources. What is substantial for you is a lot less than what is substantial for a tycoon.

What is important is that you are willing to put that substantial amount at risk by making this investment.

84. *What is meant by actively investing or being in the process of investing?*

You are doing a lot more than thinking or dreaming about it. You have made an irrevocable commitment of funds: you are not just playing around. You could lose your shirt.

85. *What if I would rather trade than invest?*

To qualify as an E-1 treaty trader you must intend to enter the U.S. temporarily solely for the purpose of carrying on substantial trade, principally between the U.S. and your home country.

86. *I have in mind a planeload of personal computers from my country to the U.S. Is that substantial trade?*

No. A one shot deal is not substantial trade. The trade has to be continuous, a stream rather than a balloon full of water. There must be numerous transactions, not just one or two big ones.

87. *What does it mean for the trade to be principally between the U.S. and my home country?*

The rule of thumb is that over 50% of the international trade from your U.S. office must be with your home country.

88. *As with the H-1B, do I have to file a petition with I.N.S.?*

No. The E-1 and E-2 have nothing to do with I.N.S. This is strictly a matter for the U.S. State Department, and you must persuade the consular officer at the U.S. Consulate in your home country that you qualify for this visa.

89. *I was the manager of my company's home office. The company now wants me to head up its U.S. branch office. What is the visa that I need?*

For a manager or executive, the right visa is L-1, designed for intracompany transfers. The theory behind it is that we are in a global marketplace, and that high level people need to enhance international business by hopping back and forth from the home country to the U.S.

90. *What do I show to qualify for this visa?*

You show that you are entering the U.S. to work in a capacity that is managerial or executive, or involves something called specialized knowledge (the tricks of the trade, where your company has something like the formula for Coca-Cola, and you are able to keep the secret and keep the competition off balance).

91. *I just started working as the manager six months ago. Do I qualify for the L-1 visa?*

No. You have to have been working continuously for one out of the last three years as a manager or executive.

92. *Can I work for a year for company A, and then take my managerial know-how to the U.S. to work for company B?*

No. You have to have worked for one out of the last three years for the very same company that you will be working for (or its parent, affiliate, or subsidiary) in the U.S.

93. *Can I get the l-1 visa on my own?*

No. You need a lawyer who can discuss details with you and with the home office of the company, to make sure that you put your best foot forward in claiming managerial or executive qualification. Use a professional if you want this visa.

94. *I have been working as the conductor of a symphony orchestra in my home country. I have a job offer from an American orchestra to be their conductor for a few years. Can I get a visa that will enable me to accept this job offer?*

Yes. The Immigration Act of 1990 introduced a new visa, called the 0-1 visa, for persons who have *extraordinary ability* in any one of five fields of endeavor.

95. *What are the 0-1 visa fields of endeavor?*

They are: Sciences, Arts, Education, Business and Athletics. We will meet these five categories again when we discuss how an employer can help you get a permanent job and an immigrant (permanent stay) visa on the basis of your extraordinary ability.

96. *How do I show that I am really extraordinary in one of these fields?*

You have to prove that you have been acclaimed for your accomplishments, and that you have either a national or international reputation. You cannot be famous just in a city or a region of your home country: your acclaim has to be at least nationwide.

97. *What does the I.N.S. want to see?*

Your prospective employer files the Form I-129 petition, and shows copies of your educational degrees, commendations from your former mentors, and the favorable publicity that has, we hope, followed you up the ladder of your career.

I.N.S. will decide the petition. If it is approved, it is sent to the U.S. Consulate in your home country for issuance of the visa.

98. *Can I come to the U.S. with the 0-1 visa, and then decide that I really want to settle down and write a novel?*

Write the novel, but do it on your own time. That's not what the visa is for.

The 0-1 visa is to enable you to continue the very kind of work, symphony orchestra conducting, that brought you acclaim and merited the extraordinary ability visa.

99. *Does the U.S. have to get anything out of this?*

Definitely. The Attorney General (in effect, I.N.S.) has to be persuaded that your entry will prospectively (in the future) benefit the U.S., and that the benefit will be substantial.

In addition to doing a fine job as the orchestra's conductor, you should consider doing some volunteer work in the community, such as visiting and conducting student orchestras at public schools.

100. *I coach the basketball team that won the national championships in my home country last month. We have the possibility of a contract with a sports impresario to visit the U.S. and play the competition there. What kind of visa do my players need to get?*

The new visa, brought in by the Immigration Act of 1990, that is called the P-1 visa, and that is designed for the athlete, entertainer, and performing artist.

101. *Why do my players qualify for it?*

They are part of a team that performs at an internationally recognized level. They seek to enter the U.S. temporarily for the purpose of taking part in a specific event.

102. *Can I do this myself, and get my players the visas that they need?*

For both the extraordinary ability O-1, and the specific performance P-1, a good immigration lawyer will do it faster and better than you can, and we recommend that you use one.

103. *I am a musician working in a remote part of my home country with ancient traditions associated with just one tribe, and not widely known throughout my country. Is there any kind of visa that I might qualify for?*

Maybe so, but you have to persuade a U.S. impresario to hire you to give a performance in the U.S.

If you have that invitation, then you may qualify for the visa that is called P-3, and that shows that the immigration law is becoming attuned to some of the world's diverse cultures and arts.

104. *What do I need to show to qualify for the P-3 visa?*

First, that your entry to the U.S. and performance will be part of a reciprocal program between the U.S. and your home country. Second, that what you have to offer as a musician is culturally unique.

105. *How does the immigration law define an artistic expression that is culturally unique?*

It is defined as a style of artistic expression, methodology, or medium that is unique to a particular country, nation, society, class, ethnicity, religion, tribe, or other group of persons.

Photocopy comments on your music and its traditions from musicologists and music critics to back up your own description of what it is that you do.

Good luck. The American public could no doubt benefit from an expansion of our musical horizons.

106. *I met a wonderful young woman when I was taking a summer course in a foreign country last year. We would like to get married. Is there anything that I can do to help her enter the U.S. and get a green card?*

Let me answer with a question: are you a U.S. citizen?

107. *Yes, I am a U.S. citizen.*

Good. If you are a U.S. citizen and have a foreign citizen fiancee, she may be just right for the K-1 nonimmigrant visa.

Once she gets that visa, she can enter the U.S., you can promptly get married here, and she can immediately apply to adjust status to legal residence. If she has children from a previous marriage or romance, they can join her in K-2 nonimmigrant status.

108. *How does she qualify for the visa?*

You and your fiancee must have met in person within the last two years. You must have the firm intention to marry within ninety days of her admission to the U.S. in K-1 status.

109. *Do I have to file a petition for my fiancee?*

Yes. You are the petitioner, she is the beneficiary, and you file the Form I-129F Petition for Alien Fiance(e), with payment of $75 fee to I.N.S. If approved, it will be sent to the U.S. Consulate in your fiancee's home country.

110. *Is it treated by the consular officer like any other application for a temporary stay (nonimmigrant) visa?*

No. Since this so-called nonimmigrant visa is actually going to convert before too long into legal residence, the consular officer will treat it as if it were the application for an immigrant (permanent stay) visa.

Therefore, the consular officer will want to make sure that your fiancee is admissible to the U.S. for a permanent stay (for example, no criminal record, no H.I.V. or other medical ground for exclusion, no public charge problem).

111. *Getting back to the requirement that we have met within the past two years. What if my fiancee is from a country, and culture, that prohibits a personal meeting with me until the day of the marriage?*

In that case, the requirement of a personal meeting will be waived. You must provide evidence that this prohibition exists, by means of a letter from the religious official who knows about the prohibition, and will preside at the formal marriage service in the U.S.

If you are asking for a waiver of the personal meeting requirement, you must of course go ahead and be married with all of the formality that you say is the reason for the personal meeting prohibition.

You cannot ask for a waiver on the basis of the formal religious requirements of your country and culture, and then get married in City Hall!

112. *My fiancee has a child in her home country, as the result of a romance several years ago. Can her child get the benefit of my petition for her, and get a visa?*

Yes. The child will be given a K-2 visa (dependent of K-1 visa holder) at the same time that your fiancee is given her K-1 visa, provided that she presents proper evidence of maternity.

113. *How soon after my fiancee's admission to the U.S. must we get married?*

With the K-1 visa stamped in her passport, your fiancee must marry you (not some other person!) within ninety days of her admission by the immigration officer at the port of entry.

114. *How soon after that can she apply for adjustment of status to legal resident?*

She can and should file her Form 1-485 Application to Adjust Status immediately after the marriage.

115. *Does she have to pay the whopping new fee of $780 that I have heard about?*

No. Since she is a nonimmigrant, and in valid status, she can pay the former fee of $130 to file her application, plus the costs of medical exam, fingerprints, and photographs.

116. *If I.N.S. required her to have a medical exam in connection with my Form 1-130 petition for her, does she need another exam in connection with her application for adjustment?*

No. One medical exam is enough.

117. *Can my spouse get work authorization while waiting for her adjustment interview?*

Yes. She files the new Form 1-765 (Rev. 4/25/95) Application for Employment Authorization with payment of $70 to I.N.S., fingerprints and photos, at the I.N.S. Center specified in the instructions. She writes (c)(5) (K-1 fiancee or K-2) at box 16, and encloses proof of filing the Form 1-485. The Employment Authorization Document (E.A.D.), which she picks up or receives by mail, will be valid for one year.

4

Will the I.N.S. Keep You Out?

When for the first time you arrive at the U.S. port of entry with your home country passport and U.S. visa, you may or may not be admitted to the U.S. by the immigration officer who is looking you over. Indeed, when you went to the U.S. Consulate in your home country to get a visa, there may have been reasons for the consular officer to refuse to issue the visa.

If you are turned away by I.N.S. at the port of entry, you will either be persuaded to return at once to your home country (this is called withdrawing your application for admission and taking voluntary departure), or will be placed under what are called exclusion proceedings and scheduled for a hearing before an immigration judge. If that happens, you will need a good immigration lawyer as soon as possible.

This chapter will not take the place of a good lawyer. It will merely highlight some of the problems you may have when you apply for a visa, or when you later apply at the port of entry for admission to the U.S., or when you still later apply for adjustment to legal resident status.

---

1. *What documents do I need to be able to travel to the U.S., and then be admitted by the Immigration and Naturalization Service?*

You need a passport from the country of which you are a citizen and, unless you are eligible for the Visa Waiver Program, a visa issued by the U.S. Consulate in that country. The period of validity of the passport must be at least six months past the period of initial stay that the I.N.S. gives you when you are admitted at the port of entry.

2. *What are the different occasions when the U.S. Consulate in my home country decides whether or not to issue me a visa?*

There are two kinds of visas: one for a temporary stay in the U.S., and one for permanent residence in the U.S. The visa for a temporary stay is called a nonimmigrant visa. The visa for a permanent stay is called an immigrant visa. When you apply for either of them, the consular officer will determine whether or not you qualify for the visa.

3. *If the U.S. Consulate denies my application for a visa, can I appeal that denial to any superior body or court?*

No, you cannot appeal a visa denial. If the consular officer denies your visa application, that decision is final. You have no way of appealing it to a superior body in the State Department, or to a court. The most that you can do is ask the consular officer's supervisor to review the decision. Review by the supervisor is optional: it is not required. For this reason, you must be familiar with the obstacles that you might run into in applying for a visa, and try to get over them before you have your visa interview.

4. *If the consular officer in my home country issues me a visa, doesn't that mean that I can come to the U.S. and be admitted by I.N.S.?*

No. Having a visa in your hand issued by the U.S. Consulate in your home country only gives you the right to arrive at the U.S. port of entry (usually the international airport where you land in the U.S.). Whether you will be admitted is up to the immigration officer who is stationed at the port of entry.

5. *What are the different occasions when the I.N.S. looks me over and decides whether to let me in or shut me out?*

Here are some of the times when you have to show I.N.S. that you are what is called admissible to the United States:

- When you arrive at the port of entry in the U.S. with a temporary stay visa (nonimmigrant visa), and are what is called an *applicant for admission;*
- When you arrive at the port of entry in the U.S. with a permanent stay visa (immigrant visa), and are, again, an applicant for admission;
- When you are already in the U.S., and have filed an application for adjustment of status to become a legal resident;
- After you get your green card, when you try to reenter the U.S. after a departure (there is a narrow exception to this rule that we will discuss later, see Question 17).

On each of these occasions, you have to show that you are admissible to the U.S., and not the opposite of admissible, which is called *excludable.*

6. *If the immigration officer at the port of entry decides not to admit me, can I appeal that decision?*

The answer is "No," if you arrived without a visa because you qualify for the Visa Waiver Program. If you arrive in that program, you waive the right to challenge the decision of the immigration officer. You can and will be sent back on the next plane to your home country.

If you arrive with a visa, and the immigration officer decides not to admit you, you will either be persuaded to withdraw your application for admission and return home on the next plane, or be placed under what are called exclusion proceedings, to see whether you should be admitted to the U.S., or excluded and sent back to your home country. To place you in proceedings, you will be served with Form I-122 Applicant for Admission Detained/Deferred for Hearing before Immigration Judge. In these proceedings, you can renew your application for admission before the immigration judge, and you will certainly need a good immigration lawyer at that time.

There is no way to appeal the decision of the immigration officer at the port of entry to a higher body within the immigration service.

7. *I am scheduled for an immigrant visa interview at the U.S. Consulate. I have multiple sclerosis, and am in a wheel chair. Will this give me trouble getting a visa and being admitted to the U.S. by I.N.S.?*

No. You are physically disabled. But physical disability is not a ground for exclusion (but watch out for the public charge ground of exclusion, if you are entering with an immigrant visa for permanent stay).

The immigration law uses the term *physical or mental disorder,* rather than disability. And it makes it clear that it is only a behavior harmful to you or another that could be a ground for exclusion. You might be inadmissible, for example, if you had a mental disorder that expressed itself through violent behavior that puts others at risk.

Multiple sclerosis, which slows you down but poses no risk to yourself or others, is obviously not such a disorder. You will get your visa and will be admitted to the U.S. by I.N.S.

8. *I am scheduled for an adjustment of status interview at I.N.S. I have been living in the U.S. for ten years. I have a U.S. citizen wife and two young U.S. citizen children. I have been trained as a computer programmer, and have a letter from a leading local business which promises to give me a job as soon as I adjust to legal status. But I have a problem. I just had my medical exam with an I.N.S.-approved doctor, and I am H.I.V.-positive. Will I be able to adjust status and get a green card?*

No, unless you get a waiver of inadmissibility.

An H.I.V.-positive reaction (H.I.V. is the virus that leads to A.I.D.S.) means that you have what the immigration law calls a communicable disease of public health significance, and that makes you excludable. Keep in mind that there are some false positives, and you should have the test re-taken by a different doctor to see whether you can get a bona fide negative result. But if a second test confirms the positive result, be aware that there is at least the possibility of a waiver of your inadmissibility, if there are very positive factors in your favor.

You might qualify for a waiver if you have one of these relationships to a person in legal immigration status:

You are the spouse, or unmarried son or daughter of any age, or minor (under twenty-one) lawfully adopted child, of a U.S. citizen, or legal resident, or foreign citizen who has been issued an immigrant visa (visa for permanent stay).

The law goes on to say that you might be eligible also if you have a son or daughter (married or unmarried, under twenty-one or twenty-one and over), who is a U.S. citizen, legal resident, or has been issued an immigrant visa.

As the spouse of a U.S. citizen, and father of two U.S. citizen children, you might very well be eligible for a waiver.

Get yourself a good immigration lawyer and make an application for a waiver of excludability. The I.N.S. form that you use for this is Form 1-601 Application for Waiver of Grounds of Excludability. The fee is $95 payable by check or money order to "Immigration and Naturalization Service." You should file for the waiver at the same time that you file your Form 1-485 Application to Adjust Status.

9. *Will I have a public charge problem if I test H.I.V.-positive?*

Yes, you might have that problem. An applicant for an immigrant visa or adjustment must satisfy the examiner that he or she is not likely, in the future, to become a public charge (be unable to be self-supporting, and become dependent on public financial assistance). Warning: There is no waiver of the public charge ground of inadmissibility.

The fact that you have a letter from a business firm that plans to employ you as soon as you adjust status is very positive. You should try to find out whether your employer's health insurance policy, once you are employed, will cover you for treatment related to your H.I.V.-positive condition.

10. *I am scheduled for an immigrant visa interview as a result of the petition for me by my wife, who is a legal resident of the U.S. As a University student in my home country, I smoked marijuana from time to time, like a lot of my friends. Will this give me any kind of a problem?*

Yes. If the interviewer asks about it, and you give the answer suggested by your question, you will have a problem. Warning: there is no waiver of inadmissibility if you are regarded as a drug abuser or addict.

I will start by assuming that you do not consider yourself to be a drug abuser or addict, and that you answered "No" when you were asked whether you were on your application for an immigrant visa. The Consulate now has that application, and your answer, in its file. The question now is: do you, from the point of view of the consular officer who may subject you to questioning at the interview, fit the immigration law definition of drug abuser or addict?

11. *How does the immigration law define drug abuser or addict?*

Here's the definition of drug abuser or addict that has been adopted by I.N.S. on the basis of regulations issued by the Public Health Service: a drug abuser or addict is someone who engages in the nonmedical use of a controlled substance (the best known examples are marijuana, heroin, cocaine, and crack cocaine, but there are others, such as amphetamines and barbiturates).

12. *But how does the law define a nonmedical use of a controlled substance?*

Nonmedical use is defined in this way: "Nonmedical use is considered more than experimentation with the substance (e.g., a single use of marijuana or other nonprescribed psychoactive substance such as amphetamines or barbiturates)."

The bottom line: if you tried marijuana once, you are admissible. If you tried it "from time to time," you have crossed over the only-one-use barrier, and you are inadmissible. If you come right out and say that to your interviewer, he or she may feel that your visa application must be denied. Consider this only-one-use barrier carefully as you prepare for your interview. We hope that the question does not come up during the interview, and that the consular officer will be satisfied with the "No" answer on your visa application.

13. *I have been a legal resident of the U.S. for five years, and am now twenty-five years old. I pleaded guilty to income tax evasion a couple of years ago, and was given a suspended sentence. I am now planning a long trip to my home country to visit my family. Will I have a problem getting back into the U.S.?*

Yes, you will (if I.N.S. is efficient and has learned of your conviction).

You may think that you have paid your debt to society by pleading guilty and getting a suspended sentence, and that you are now as free as a bird. But that's not the way the immigration law works. You have been convicted of (or pleaded guilty to, which amounts to the same thing) what the law calls a crime of moral turpitude, and that makes you excludable. When you seek to reenter the U.S., you will be stopped at the port of entry and placed under exclusion proceedings.

14. *How does the immigration law define a crime of moral turpitude?*

It can either be a crime of violence, like robbery, rape, or murder, or it can be a non-violent crime of dishonesty, or so-called bad behavior.

The word turpitude means something base or vile, as defined by community standards. In the U.S., cheating the government and anybody else is considered that kind of crime (even though some people do it and get away with it). You did not physically harm anybody by evading your tax payments, but the immigration law treats you as severely as if you did. The non-violent crimes of moral turpitude include income tax evasion, welfare fraud, Medicaid fraud, food stamp fraud, and shoplifting.

Other non-violent bad behavior offenses that constitute moral turpitude crimes include prostitution or procuring prostitution (that is, arranging for women to become prostitutes, and extracting a portion of their proceeds). Prostitution, of course, includes male prostitution and child prostitution.

15. *Is there any exception to being excludable as the result of committing a crime of moral turpitude?*

Yes, there is an exception, but it is a narrow one.

If you were convicted of a crime of moral turpitude (only one crime) when you were under age eighteen, and if five years went by from the time you committed the crime or were released from confinement (if you were imprisoned), then you would not be excludable for having committed a crime of moral turpitude.

You would not be stopped at the port of entry and turned back, and your application for an immigrant visa or for adjustment of status would not be denied on the basis of the crime. Your youth at the time of the crime, and the passage of time, would shield you from being excluded.

But from what you have said in our imaginary case, you were over eighteen when you committed the crime of moral turpitude, and so are not within the exception.

16. *If I do not qualify for this narrow exception, is there a waiver that I might qualify for?*

There is, but only if you are the spouse, parent, or child (whether under twenty-one or twenty-one and over, unmarried or married) of a U.S. citizen or legal resident, and if that close relative would suffer extreme hardship if you were excluded. Look back to chapter 3, Question 41 for information on how to show extreme hardship if deported (the same difficulties exist in showing hardship if excluded).

You are unmarried. You do not qualify for the waiver. You will be placed under exclusion proceedings, and I.N.S. will try to have you sent back to your home country. You need to confer with a good immigration lawyer to see whether you have any way out of what seems to be a blind alley.

17. *But what if my mother has just died and I absolutely must go home for the funeral. I will only be staying outside the U.S. for three days. Under those circumstances, can't I get back into the U.S.?*

Now I see a glimmer of hope for you.

You may fit a narrow exception to the general rule that I.N.S. will look you over every time that you try to enter the U.S. A U.S. Supreme Court case in 1963 by the name of *Fleuti* established this rule: you will not be looked over and checked for excludability if your departure was brief, casual, and innocent, and did not meaningfully interrupt your lawful permanent residence. If the I.N.S. makes an error and stops you at the border, have your lawyer make what is called a *Fleuti* motion, arguing that your return from a brief visit did not make an "entry" (I know, it doesn't make sense to a non-lawyer, but your lawyer may be able to take advantage of this valuable rule).

18. *I am a gay (homosexual) man. I intend to apply for a temporary stay (non-immigrant) visa to visit the U.S. for a while. Will the fact that I am gay make it impossible for me to get a visa?*

No. It will have no impact on your qualification to get a visa, either a temporary stay (nonimmigrant) or permanent stay (immigrant) visa.

A few years ago my answer would have been different. The immigration law formerly excluded foreign citizens described as afflicted with psychopathic personality, or sexual deviation, or mental defect. Homosexuality was at that time considered to be both psychopathic and a sexual deviation, and it was one of the questions that consular officers sometimes asked of visa applicants. This is now ancient history. The only thing left of these grounds of exclusion is mental defect, and that applies only if the defect is connected with behavior that is harmful to the foreign citizen or to another person.

However, I have a word of caution for you. There are immigration examiners who were trained under the old system, when homosexuality was a bar. They may still have a mind-set that dates back to that era. Your sexual orientation is not now relevant to your admissibility, and I suggest that you do not bring it up, either. Both you and your interviewer should stick to what is relevant to your admissibility.

19. *I was born and brought up in one of the Eastern European countries that used to be under communist rule. As a high school student, I was required, in order to graduate, to become a member of the Communist Party. I am now scheduled for a visa interview on the basis of an approved petition filed for me by my U.S. citizen spouse. Will I have any trouble getting a visa?*

Not if you give persuasive testimony to spell out why you were forced to become a communist.

The general rule is that you will be inadmissible for permanent residence if you were ever a member of, or affiliated with, the Communist Party of any country. Note: the bar against communists no longer applies if you are coming for a short stay with a nonimmigrant visa.

There is an exception for immigrants, however, if you were a member involuntarily, or only while under age sixteen, or if you had to be a member to obtain employment, food rations, or other essentials of living. In your case, membership was involuntary: it was the price of graduating from high school, which was no doubt essential to getting a job and surviving economically. Enclose an affidavit with your application for a visa, and emphasize (if true) your antipathy to communism, the pain it caused you to become a party member, and your hope to soon be able to be admitted to a country where the government does not enforce a political belief on its citizens.

20. *If a foreign citizen is a member of a terrorist organization, can he get a visa and be admitted to the United States?*

This answer may surprise you. It is "Yes."

The law does not forbid the grant of a visa and admission to the U.S. of a foreign citizen who is merely a member of a terrorist organization. To be denied a visa and admission, the consular officer or immigration officer must know, or at least have reason to believe, that the foreign citizen is "engaged in terrorist activities," which must mean something more than mere membership.

When some politicians instantly assumed, without any factual basis, that the tragic bombing in Oklahoma City in April, 1995 was the work of foreign terrorists, a Senator proposed to amend the immigration law to exclude foreign citizens who were members of a terrorist organization.

Given the determination of Congress to combat terrorism, both domestic and foreign, it seems likely that this provision of the immigration law will be changed.

21. *I have been in the U.S. for three years. I came as a visitor, and then overstayed my period of authorized stay. I am now scheduled for an adjustment of status interview as the result of a petition filed for me by my legal resident spouse. I have worked off and on as a baby sitter and waitress, but do not now have a steady job. Am I going to have a problem with my adjustment application?*

You might very well have a problem. The law states that you are not admissible if the consular officer or immigration officer (in your case it is the immigration officer) believes that you are likely, at any time in the future, to become what is called a public charge, which means someone who will have to go on welfare (get public cash assistance) in order to survive. Warning: There is no waiver of the public charge ground of exclusion. If the immigration officer believes that you will have to go on welfare, you will not be able to adjust status and become a legal resident.

The immigration officer will take a look at the so-called Poverty Guidelines that are published each year by the U.S. Department of Health and Human Services, and will use them as a guide to see whether you are or are not above the poverty line.

For 1995, the guidelines noted that you would be over the poverty threshold if you earned more than: $7,470 for a family unit of one; $10,030 for a family unit of two; $12,590 for a family unit of three; $15,150 for a family unit of four; $17,710 for a family unit of five; $20,270 for a family unit of six; $22,830 for a family unit of seven; $25,390 for a family unit of eight. Add $2,560 for each additional family member.

These guidelines apply to all states except for Alaska and Hawaii, where the poverty threshold levels are considerably higher, and they apply to the District of Columbia.

Before you have your adjustment interview, you should make every effort to obtain a job offer, and get a notarized letter from your future employer stating that you will be employed at a certain rate of pay once you are adjusted and thereby eligible to work legally.

If you cannot get such a job offer letter, your spouse must submit a Form I-134 Affidavit of Support. In the affidavit, he states that his income will be "deemed" a part of yours for three years after you have adjusted, from the point of view of your eligibility to obtain any form of public cash assistance. The purpose of this is to make it impossible for low income persons who adjust on the basis of a petition by a close relative to immediately go on welfare, and impose a cost on the U.S. taxpayer. Some proposals now pending in Congress would extend that "deeming" period from three years to five years, to continue the obligation of the sponsoring relative, not the government, to support the new legal resident. Others would continue the "deeming" responsibility until the person admitted as a legal resident becomes a U.S. citizen.

22. *If I leave the U.S. for a trip back home before the I.N.S. decides my adjustment application, is that a problem?*

Yes. If you leave the U.S. while your application is pending, you will have abandoned the adjustment application. The approved petition that was filed for you by your close relative may still be valid, and you must (with your lawyer) try to get I.N.S. to forward the approved petition to the U.S. Consulate in your home country, so that you can have an interview there for an immigrant visa. But that's a very round-about way of proceeding. Just observe this rule: while your adjustment application is pending, do not depart from the United States!

23. *I entered the U.S. six years ago with a fake passport and visa, in someone else's* *name. The I.N.S. officer at the port of entry did not notice anything wrong, and I was admitted. I have been working as a baby-sitter ever since, and am now making pretty good money. I met and fell in love with a legal resident of the U.S., and we are now married. Is there anything that my husband can do to help me get a green card?*

We need to think this over carefully, and you need to consult with a good immigration lawyer.

The first point is this: you used fraud to obtain documentation and to enter the U.S. This is called misrepresentation, and makes you inadmissible. The second point is that there may be at least the possibility of a waiver of your inadmissibility.

If the misrepresentation occurred at least ten years before you apply for adjustment, and if you have a spouse who is a legal resident or U.S. citizen, and if the Attorney General (in effect, I.N.S.) determines that your admission would not be contrary to national welfare, safety, or security, you may be able to get a waiver of inadmissibility, and be adjusted to legal residence.

What is your best approach? As we will discover further on in chapter 8, you cannot adjust until an immigrant visa is immediately available to you. It might be best to sit back for a while, and wait for your husband to be eligible to apply for naturalization (look ahead to chapter 20). Once he is a citizen, you are what is called an immediate relative, and right away his petition for you may be accompanied by your application for adjustment, which you file at the same time.

The waiver application is filed on Form 1-601 Application for Waiver of Grounds of Excludability, with fee of $95 to "Immigration and Naturalization Service." You file it at the same time that you file your Form 1-485 Application to Adjust Status. Be prepared to pay the new adjustment fee of $780 (refer ahead to chapter 8).

24. *I hear there are some tough new penalties for document fraud. Is that going to be an additional problem for me?*

Not if I.N.S. grants your Form 1-601 Application for a Waiver of Excludability.

Here's how it works. Your spouse (now a U.S. citizen) files the Form 1-130 Petition for Alien Relative for you, and you file the Form 1-485 Application to Adjust Status for yourself. With that application, you file the Form 1-601 Application for a Waiver of Excludability, on the basis of your marriage to a U.S. citizen and his petition for you.

If I.N.S. grants the waiver, it will also approve your application for adjustment, and your worries will be over. The Service does not want to be in the odd position of starting proceedings for document fraud, when it has just waived that very ground of excludability.

If I.N.S. denies your waiver application, it will also deny the adjustment application. At that point, I.N.S. may start a document fraud proceeding against you.

25. *I was deported a year ago because I had overstayed and I.N.S. caught up with* *me. My wife back in America is now a U.S. citizen and would like to file a petition for me. How soon can I get back into the U.S.?*

Not as soon as you think.

Once you have been deported, you may not enter the U.S. on the basis of a petition filed for you by a close relative for five years, unless the Attorney General (in effect, I.N.S.) gives you permission to do so. Get yourself a good immigration lawyer, or, since you are not here, suggest that your spouse get one. With a legal resident or U.S. citizen spouse speaking up for you, you may be able to persuade I.N.S. to be flexible and to "give you a break."

26. *I have a friend who was stopped at the port of entry, placed under exclusion proceedings, and sent back. But he got back to the U.S. in about a year. Why the big difference?*

The rules are different for someone sent back after losing a deportation case, and someone sent back after losing an exclusion case. I gather that your friend has a U.S. citizen spouse who petitioned for him, otherwise there would be no way to return to the U.S. that soon.

The person excluded and sent back cannot return for a year. The person who is deported cannot return for five years. It may not make sense to you, but it is the law and you have to know about it and keep it in mind. And get yourself a good immigration lawyer if you need to persuade I.N.S., either in the exclusion or deportation context, to make an exception to the rule in your case.

5

Political Asylum

In 1980 the U.S. Congress passed a law called the Refugee Act that defined the term refugee, and stated that the Attorney General (in effect, the I.N.S.) would adopt procedures making it possible for persons in the U.S. to apply for asylum if they had been persecuted or had a well-founded fear of persecution in their home countries.

A key idea of the asylum law is that persons who have stuck their necks out in their home countries by expressing an opinion that their government wishes to punish them for will not be forced back to their home countries, where government agents may be seeking to do them harm. And it is not only a matter of having and expressing an opinion: there may be some characteristic that the person has that may lead to being targeted for persecution by the government.

Since a key purpose of asylum is to help vulnerable people, regulations also made it possible for asylum applicants to obtain work authorization while their cases were pending. Neither the asylum application nor the request for work authorization cost anything (this is still the rule), and in this sense asylum was and is extremely generous, since virtually all the other applications to the I.N.S. require a fee.

The public's attitude toward immigrants has hardened in recent years, however, and we will see in this chapter that new rules adopted by I.N.S. in December, 1994 make the road rougher for anyone who wishes to apply for asylum.

In the discussion that follows, we will move from one imaginary situation to another. We will not cover all of the possible reasons to file an asylum application, but will give a sketch of some of the different kinds of claims that may lead to a grant of asylum.

It is important to get a good immigration lawyer to help you to evaluate the strengths and weaknesses of your case. If there is merit to it, your lawyer will be able to accentuate what is positive about it. An asylum application is not something that you should try to do by yourself.

Nevertheless, we will give a bird's eye view of the procedure, and you may recognize yourself in one or another of our imaginary examples.

---

1. *I am a citizen of Cuba. I have had a lot of trouble with the government, which knows me as an opponent of the regime. Can I apply for asylum right here in Cuba, or do I have to get on a rickety boat and risk the trip to Miami, and apply for asylum there?*

Don't risk the trip. Even if you survive the passage, you will almost certainly be picked up by the U.S. Coast Guard and, according to a new U.S. policy, sent back to Cuba unless a shipboard interview reveals that you have a valid persecution claim.

The general rule is that a person who is afraid of persecution at home has to be outside of the home country in order to apply for asylum. However, an exception was briefly made for Haitians during 1994, when a blockade prevented them from fleeing, and a brutal military regime kept them terrified. For a few months, they were permitted to apply for asylum at the U.S. Consulate in the capital city.

Another exception to the general rule was worked out September 9, 1994 between the U.S. and Cuba, in the wake of the flood of persons fleeing for the U.S. in boats, rafts, and inner tubes during the summer of 1994. If you fear persecution from your government, you may now undertake what is called in-country asylum processing. You may go to the U.S. Interests Section in Havana and submit your application there. Your case will be a good one if you have been a political prisoner, or experienced religious persecution, or forced labor, or other inhumane treatment.

Your spouse and unmarried children under age twenty-one will be granted asylum with you. If you have other close family members who live in your household, they may be granted what is called humanitarian parole, to enable them to enter the U.S. with you, which will make it possible for them to adjust status to legal residence a year later. To get an up-to-date description of this special asylum program, call I.N.S. at its toll-free number 1-800-755-0777.

2. *I am a student in F-1 status. After I left my home country, which is a democracy, a coup ousted the President and installed a military dictatorship. Does this give me a reason to apply for asylum?*

Yes. I cannot say that you will win your asylum case, but you certainly have a reason to make the application.

Military regimes generally are very suspicious of students, since students are more likely than some other groups to stand up and protest against dictatorships. When they organize and protest, they are likely to be arrested, interrogated, sometimes tortured and even killed.

To evaluate the strength of your case, your lawyer will need to know more about you and your own past history and beliefs, and a lot more about the military coup and its aftermath. Has the military regime already started to go after student leaders?

But, for the moment, we can say that it is certainly worth considering making an application for asylum.

3. *Can I apply for asylum while I am still in student status, or do I have to wait until I am out of status?*

Yes, you can apply for asylum while you are still in valid student status, and no, you do not have to wait until your status expires.

The asylum law says that someone who is in the U.S. can apply for asylum irrespective of status (regardless of status). This means that you can be in valid student status, or your status may have expired, or you may have violated your status by working more than twenty hours per week, or by not maintaining a full course of studies.

Indeed, this rule applies to someone who neve. was in valid status: someone, for example, who crossed the border with Mexico or Canada and entered the U.S. without having been inspecced by an immigration offic

Whether you are in valid temporary stay (nonimmigrant) status, or are out of status, or are someone who entered illegally, you have a right to apply for asylum.

4. *If I apply for asylum, does that have the effect of cancelling my F-1 student status?*

No. So long as you continue to be a student taking a full course of studies, and complying with the rules concerning student employment, you will remain in valid F-1 status. Your application for asylum will not affect that valid status in any way.

5. *If my asylum application is rejected, will my student status be cancelled?*

No. One application has nothing to do with the other. So long as you stay in valid student status, that status will continue. A rejection of your asylum application does not cancel your student status.

6. *What do I have to show to merit a grant of asylum?*

You have to show that you are a refugee.

7. *How does the law define a refugee?*

As someone who is outside of the home country, and unable to safely return to that country, either because they have been persecuted, or have a well-founded fear of persecution in the future.

8. *What does it mean to be persecuted?*

To be persecuted is to be pursued, to be hounded, to be tracked down, the way a fox is pursued by hounds, during a hunt. The government is the hunter, and you are the hunted. The government seeks to do you harm.

Let's imagine an example. You lead a peaceful and well publicized demonstration to protest the policies of the dictator of your country. The government denounces the demonstration in the media as being inspired by a foreign power, and the military police track down and kill one of your fellow student leaders.

You fear, for good reason, that you could be next. This is a well-founded fear of persecution.

9. *What are the different reasons for being persecuted?*

There are five listed in the Refugee Act. In the example just given, where you led a demonstration to protest government policies, the basis for the government's persecution of you is your political opinion.

The five bases noted in the law are: race, religion, nationality, membership in a particular social group, or political opinion.

10. *Does the persecutor always have to be the government?*

No, although the government must be at least allowing or "turning a blind eye" to the persecution. If the persecutor is not the government itself, it must be an individual or group that the government is unwilling or unable to control. But remember: the reason for the persecution has to be one of the five reasons listed in the law.

11. *What if there is a "death squad" in my home country that is killing opponents of the government, but the government insists that it knows nothing about it?*

If the government and the "death squad" are targeting the same opponents, you have reason to fear that the "death squad" is doing the government's bidding, and the government is not being honest when it says it knows nothing about its activities.

This would be a good example of a group that the government is unable or unwilling to control. The "death squad" is like an agent of the government, and persecution by the "death squad" is interchangeable with persecution by the government.

12. *What if one of my neighbors back home has sworn to kill me if he ever sees me again in my home country?*

That is not persecution. It is a violent personal dispute. It cannot serve as the basis for an asylum claim.

13. *What if that neighbor is a leading member of the town council in my home town?*

It still sounds more like a personal dispute than persecution. It would only be if the town council, as a body, were to go after you because of some political opinion that you have (or one of the other four listed reasons) that we might start to think that this could amount to persecution.

But there's another problem. The asylum law suggests that persecution must be country-wide, not localized. If the only organ of government that is hounding you is your town council, that may be too local. Even if you have lived all your life in that town, the asylum officer or immigration judge may think that you should just move to another town, and so be out of the zone of persecution.

14. *I am a women, and a writer. I have criticized the laws and customs of my country that forbid women from obtaining a higher education, and practicing a profession. Does that give me a reason to fear persecution?*

It may. Your lawyer needs to do some hard work and find out how your government has reacted in the recent past to women who have spoken out as you have.

If a member of the press criticizes your writing and condemns your opinion, that is worrisome but not necessarily a grave danger (unless the newspaper is an official government newspaper). But if a member of the government condemns you as a "feminist" and a "danger to our way of life," you can then anticipate serious trouble, and your claim to asylum is much more urgent. It may, indeed, be a matter of life or death.

15. *I was not involved in political matters. However, my husband in the home country has been abusing me for years. I managed to get a tourist visa to the U.S. with my child. We overstayed, and have been placed under deportation proceedings by I.N.S. Do I have any chance of winning an asylum case?*

A year ago, the answer would have been "No." I.N.S. would have argued that this was a purely personal dispute, and was not persecution by the government or a government agent for one of the five reasons in the statute (race, religion, nationality, membership in a particular social group, or political opinion). The immigration judge would have agreed with that argument, and denied your application.

As we go to press, the answer is "Perhaps." A key question is: what did the government do about the abuse? If you tried hard to get the government to prevent or punish this abuse, and it did nothing, the judge would incline toward your claim. If the government went even further and took your husband's side, for example by a court order preventing you from leaving the country, your case would be stronger still.

16. *If the judge decides in my favor, which one of the five statutory reasons would he or she be looking at?*

Let's look at a recent case, where the applicant testified that she favored so-called Western values of the dignity of women in the marriage context. The judge decided the case on the basis of both political opinion and membership in a particular social group. The political opinion aspect of the decision rested on the applicant's belief in Western values. The social group aspect rested on the applicant's membership in a group consisting of women "who espouse Western values and are unwilling to live their lives at the mercy of their husbands, their society, their government."

This decision reflects a new and welcome development in the law.

17. *Has the I.N.S. kept up with these new developments concerning asylum claims by women?*

Yes. The old days of interpreting every form of abuse of a woman as a purely personal matter or a common crime, but not persecution, are over.

New guidelines published by I.N.S. are designed to alert asylum officers to the particular kinds of abuse of women that may form the basis for a valid claim of persecution. The strength of the claim must still be weighed on a case by case basis. But attention will now be paid to the alarming varieties of mistreatment of women, such as rape, sexual abuse and domestic violence, infanticide, and genital mutilation.

18. *I had to flee my home country, and illegally cross the border and enter the U.S. The reason I fled is that I am a gay (homosexual) man, and my home country has launched a campaign of intimidation against gay men, resulting in interrogation and imprisonment for some. Do I have any chance of winning an asylum case?*

Yes, you do. This is a recent development in the law. It can be a lifesaver for those who can build a convincing case. However, your case has to be very well supported by your own testimony, and by documentation, if possible.

One of the ironic features of the asylum law is this: the worse your treatment was in your home country (short of being killed), the better will be your chance of being granted asylum in the U.S. In one of the several cases that have been reported and decided in favor of a gay man, it was a dramatic and dreadful story. The man had been harassed by the police of his home country as a homosexual. The police also had threatened him, extorted money from him, and on one occasion he was raped by a police officer.

19. *If anything terrible like that happened to me, how could I convince the immigration service or the immigration judge that these things really had happened to me?*

Your own testimony, if it is detailed and believable, can be enough to convince the I.N.S. or the immigration judge to grant you asylum.

You are not expected to have any documents from the government stating that you have been horribly treated as a result of your sexual orientation. That's not the sort of thing that an oppressive government will ever admit to.

20. *Which of the five categories will my claim of persecution as a homosexual fit into?*

The five categories are: race, religion, nationality, membership in a particular social group, and political opinion.

Your claim of persecution as a homosexual fits into the category of membership in a particular social group.

21. *I can't show evidence from the government about my own case. Are there any other sources of evidence that might help me?*

Yes. The I.N.S. and immigration judge are interested in seeing what is called background evidence about your home country, and specifically, in your case, about whether their treatment of homosexuals is known, and is considered to be a serious violation of human rights. Your lawyer can help you get some relevant material to copy and show to the asylum officer or immigration judge.

The U.S. State Department publishes, in February of each year, a thick volume called Country Report on Human Rights Practices. Amnesty International publishes an annual report on human rights practices. The Lawyer's Committee for Human Rights publishes an annual critique of the State Department's report, and occasional reports on human rights conditions in specific countries.

All of these materials are given weight by the asylum officer or immigration judge. It is not just the State Department publication that is paid attention to.

These suggestions are not limited to cases of persecution for sexual orientation. They apply to claims of persecution for any one of the five reasons listed in the asylum law: race, religion, nationality, membership in a particular social group, or political opinion.

22. *Do I have to go to the trouble and expense of copying and presenting these materials, or can I assume that the asylum officer or immigration judge has them already, and can look these things up?*

You have to go to the trouble of presenting these materials yourself. If you do not, the asylum officer or immigration judge is allowed to conclude that there is no such documentation to back up your own testimony. That will make it much harder for you to convince the asylum officer or immigration judge that you deserve a grant of asylum.

23. *How do I file my application for asylum?*

You file the Form I-589 Request for Asylum in the United States with I.N.S. You must use the form that is dated 11/16/94 at the bottom left of the first page of instructions, and the bottom left of the first page of the seven page form itself. Older forms will not be accepted. You file the Form I-589 with the Form G-325A Biographic Information, the Form FD-258 Fingerprint chart (two samples), and two identical color photos.

There is no fee payable to I.N.S. to apply for asylum.

24. *Does my application go to the asylum officer, or to the immigration judge?*

That depends.

If you are the F-1 student whose home country government has just been overturned by a military coup, and you are not yourself under deportation proceedings, you file what is called an affirmative application. It goes to the I.N.S., which forwards it to its asylum unit and puts it in the hands of a so-called asylum officer who does nothing but consider asylum cases. The instructions to the form will tell you where it must be filed.

If you fled your country with someone else's passport and visa, you will be stopped at the port of entry by I.N.S., and placed under exclusion proceedings. You will be brought before the immigration judge soon after, and will then submit what is called a defensive application. It is then the judge, not the I.N.S., who determines the case.

If you crossed the border with Canada or Mexico, and were then picked up by I.N.S., you will be placed under deportation proceedings. Your application will then be defensive, and will be decided by the judge.

25. *How do I get work authorization?*

You submit the Form I-765 Application for Employment Authorization. There is no fee. You write box (c)(8) at box 16, and will get work authorization only if your asylum application is pending, and is nonfrivolous.

26. *What does* nonfrivolous *mean?*

It means that there is something to the application. It may not be a winning application, but it is not just hot air. If you say that you fear persecution because you had an argument with a neighbor who threatened your life, that is frivolous: a threat from a neighbor is not persecution. You will not win your asylum case, and you may not even get work authorization while your case is pending.

If you truthfully state that a government official threatened your life because you hate the President's policies, there may be something to that claim. It is, at least, nonfrivolous, and you will get work authorization.

27. *What does* pending *mean?*

Your case is pending if it has not been finally decided against you.

If you lose before the I.N.S. asylum officer, and the Service starts deportation proceedings against you, your case is still pending.

If you lose before the immigration judge, and appeal that decision, your case is still pending.

If you lose your appeal to the Board of Immigration Appeals, and appeal that decision to a Federal court, your case is still pending.

During these months or years, you can renew, and maintain, your work authorization.

28. *How soon will I get my work authorization?*

Here, life is much harder now than it was before December, 1994.

According to the new I.N.S. asylum rules, you cannot file the Form I-765 request for work authorization for 150 days after filing the Form I-589 application for asylum. After you file Form I-765, the rule states that I.N.S. will decide the work authorization request within 30 days.

The bottom line is this: no matter how good a case you have, you will have to wait about 180 days (about six months) before getting work authorization and being able to work legally in the U.S.

29. *How do I file for the Employment Authorization Document?*

I.N.S. rules require that the I-765 application be mailed to the Service Center noted in the instructions, with a copy of the I-589 asylum application and proof that is was filed with the I.N.S. or immigration court.

30. *How quickly will my employment application be decided?*

The application for employment authorization will be decided within thirty days of its receipt, and the Employment Authorization Document (E.A.D.) will be mailed to you or picked up by you, valid for one year. When the time comes to apply to renew your work authorization, I.N.S. will take up to ninety days to decide the renewal application.

31. *I am a citizen of China. I am married to a young woman who is still in China. I fled to the United States because we wish to have several children, and the government prohibits having more than one. Do I have a good case for asylum?*

I can't say. Your lawyer will have to work hard, and try to individualize your· case as much as possible. The U.S., not surprisingly, is not ready to grant asylum easily to large numbers of young Chinese men and women, merely because they do not agree with their nation's law on limited childbirth. It may also be that the U.S. is "walking on eggs" and does not wish to offend the Chinese authorities by implying, by a large-scale grant of asylum cases, that the law in question constitutes a serious violation of human rights.

Do you belong to an organization, or to a church, that objects to the law, and have the authorities taken action against that organization or church as a result of their opposition? Have you yourself been taken to task by an official, who has warned you or your wife of the dire consequences of not complying with the law?

Some asylum claims based on China's one-child-only law have been granted, many have been denied by the I.N.S. or by immigration judges. It will depend on the particular facts of your case.

32. *I have a family emergency back home: my father is dying. Can I get I.N.S. permission to travel home to see him for the last time?*

I am sorry to have to give you a "No" answer to your question.

There is a procedure to apply for what is called advance parole by filing Form I-131 Application for Travel Document, and stating that you have a family emergency. But if your father is in your home country, the very country where you say you fear persecution, a return to that country will cancel the advance parole and be an abandonment of your asylum claim as well.

33. *How long does my E.A.D. last?*

It is good for one year. After one year, if your case is still pending, you may file another Form I-765 application to extend your work authorization for another year.

34. *Will that cost me anything?*

Yes. To renew your work authorization, you must pay a fee of $70 to "Immigration and Naturalization Service."

35. *What if I make an affirmative application, but the asylum officer rejects my application?*

What happens then is that you get a second chance. The I.N.S. will place you under deportation proceedings, and you may then renew your application before the immigration judge. You have a "second bite at the apple."

36. *If the immigration judge decides against me, will I be deported right away?*

Not if you appeal the decision in a timely manner. A timely appeal will stay (put on hold) the judge's decision.

37. *How soon must I appeal a decision that goes against me?*

When the judge reads the decision and order against you in the immigration court, you (or your lawyer) will be asked whether you accept it as a final order. If you say "Yes," then you could be taken into custody by I.N.S. and promptly deported. So you, or your lawyer, answer "No," and say "we wish to appeal." The judge will then hand you three copies of the appeal form, E.O.I.R. (Executive Office for Immigration Review) 26 Notice of Appeal to the Board of Immigration Appeals, and give you a date by which you must file your appeal (it will be ten days from the date of the decision and order).

38. *Where do I file the appeal?*

If you are not in I.N.S. detention, you file at the immigration court office near the courtroom where you had your hearing. If you are in I.N.S. detention, you must file the appeal in the immigration court office near the courtroom where you had your hearing, which is near your place of detention. Do not make the mistake of filing the appeal in the court office that is used by persons who are not detained: by the time your appeal arrives in the court near your place of detention, it may be too late, and you may already have been sent back home. Be careful: this sometimes happens, even if you have a lawyer!

39. *What is the fee to appeal the decision that goes against me?*

The fee is $110. Your lawyer will know where the cashier's office for the court is located, pay the fee in cash, and get a receipt to present to the court office when filing the appeal papers. Before the court office will accept them, you (or your lawyer) must note in writing that a copy of the appeal has been served on I.N.S. at the appropriate office.

40. *Can I be excused from paying that fee?*

You can try, by making a motion to the judge who decided your case. It is called a poor person's motion (motion *in forma pauperis*), and in it you state that you are entitled to relief, but have no financial resources and cannot afford to pay the fee. This sometimes is granted, especially if you are held in detention and it is understood that you have no ability to earn a living. It helps if the government attorney does not oppose it, but that will depend on which government attorney you have.

41. *What do I put down on the appeal form itself?*

Here's where you really need a lawyer (just as you did in preparing your application and having your hearing before the judge). Your lawyer must put down several reasons why the judge's decision should be overturned when it is reviewed by the superior body called the Board of Immigration Appeals. Where did the judge make an error? If you do not state specific reasons for the appeal, it will be summarily dismissed (dismissed without considering the merits of the case), and you will find yourself heading home promptly.

42. *Does my lawyer have to write a brief within ten days?*

No. On the appeal form your lawyer states that a brief (a legal argument on your behalf) will be submitted later, when the transcript of your hearing is prepared.

43. *How long will it take to prepare the transcript of the hearing?*

If you are in I.N.S. detention, it will be prepared in a matter of weeks, because the government is eager to save the taxpayers money and get you out of the U.S. as soon as possible. If you are not in I.N.S. detention, it is likely to take months, even as long as a year. During that time, your case is still pending, and you will be permitted to apply for a renewal of work authorization, if needed.

44. *My spouse and children are back in the home country. If I am granted asylum, do they automatically get it too?*

It's not automatic. However, your spouse and children (under twenty-one and unmarried) may be able to "piggy-back" on your winning application. You file a Form 1-730 Refugee/Asylee Relative Petition with I.N.S. (no fee). That petition, if approved, will permit your spouse and children to do something that is called following to join you. This is a very useful petition. It means that you do not have to wait to get a green card, and only then be able to file a petition for your spouse and (unmarried) children.

45. *If I am granted asylum, do I get my green card at the same time?*

No. As someone granted asylum, you are called an asylee. You have to be an asylee for one year, and then you file for adjustment of status by submitting Form 1-485 and necessary documentation. You do not need to pay the usual fee to file for adjustment as a person who was granted asylum. If your spouse has followed to join you, she submits her adjustment application at the same time (see chapter 8 for information on how to file an application for adjustment).

46. *Might there be certain things in my background that could prevent me from being granted asylum?*

Yes. If you were firmly resettled in a third country before arriving in the U.S., you cannot be granted asylum. You cannot be granted asylum if you committed certain particularly serious crimes in your home country. If you committed an aggravated felony in the U.S. (such as robbery, murder, or drug trafficking) you cannot be granted asylum, no matter how strong or well-founded is your fear of persecution in your home country.

47. *Will I have a public charge problem, like everybody else applying for adjustment?*

I hope that you are able to make a living in the U.S., and that you are doing just that at the present time. However, you should know that the rules that apply to everybody else do not apply to persons granted asylum: being likely to become a public charge will not be a reason to deny your application for adjustment.

Temporary Protected Status

One of the new features of the Immigration Act of 1990 was the providing of temporary refuge in the U.S. for those who would be in danger at home. The new feature is called Temporary Protected Status (T.P.S.). It is a common sense humanitarian procedure that permits foreign citizens of countries that are torn apart by civil war or natural disaster to remain in the U.S. for a time, until the emergency is over and it is safe for the foreign citizen to return home.

It is just a temporary measure. It may be extended for a while, but it will not lead, by itself, to permanent legal residence. Even if you are in T.P.S. for several years, it does not get you any closer to legal residence.

1. *I came to the U.S. as a student, and there was recently a coup in my country that brought to power a military dictatorship. Does this qualify me for T.P.S.?*

No. Something more dramatic and terrible must have happened in your home country. An example would be the genocide that was perpetrated in the small African country of Rwanda in 1994, and that resulted in the death of a half million persons during a period of several months. That's the sort of human disaster that will lead to T.P.S for citizens of that country who are presently in the U.S..

And it's rare for a country to be designated for T.P.S. protection. Remember the situation in Haiti following the coup in 1991 that ousted the elected President? The junta that ruled the country after the coup committed human rights abuses on a large scale, including the assassination of political opponents, and these abuses went on for three years. But Haitian citizens in the U.S. were never protected by Temporary Protected Status.

2. *Who decides which countries to put on the T.P.S. list of countries?*

The Attorney General decides, after weighing the factors described in the law.

3. *What are the factors that lead to designating a country for Temporary Protected Status?*

The law requires the Attorney General to look at these emergency conditions:
- an ongoing armed conflict in the country that would pose a serious threat to its citizens, if they were forced to return home;
- earthquake, flood, drought, epidemic, or other environmental disaster resulting in a substantial, but temporary, disruption of living conditions there, if the country affected cannot handle the return of its citizens;
- an extraordinary and temporary condition that would prevent its citizens from returning in safety, unless the Attorney General finds that permitting those citizens to remain here would be against U.S. national interest.

4. *Which of those three factors caused Rwanda to be designated for T.P.S.?*

Rwanda does not exactly fit the first two factors: by the time of designation the armed conflict was over, and the epidemic had stabilized. But it certainly fits the third: extraordinary and temporary conditions that make it unsafe for its citizens to return.

It is interesting to note that genocide is not one of the factors listed in the law. Strictly speaking, the Attorney General does not have to consider it. But the nature of that crime against humanity is so grave that we hope and trust that the Attorney General will always consider it, and never deport citizens to a country where genocide is practiced by one group against members of another.

5. *How does the Attorney General make the designation known?*

It is published in the government record called the Federal Register.

6. *How long does the designation last?*
The initial designation is for a period between six and eighteen months.

7. *Can the time period be continued?*
Yes. If the emergency situation is still ongoing, it can and will be continued. If the emergency is over, the designation will be terminated.

8. *What is an example of a terminated designation?*
Citizens of Kuwait were designated once that country was invaded and occupied by Iraq several years ago. Once Iraqi forces were expelled from Kuwait in the wake of the so-called Gulf War, and the situation there had stabilized, the designation was terminated. There was no longer any risk to a Kuwaiti citizen to return to the home country.

9. *What if I am not a citizen of the country that was designated for T.P.S., but had been residing there for years, and it's where I made my living and raised my family. Do I qualify?*
Yes. If you have no citizenship, but if the designated country is where you last habitually resided (and you can prove that), then you can get the benefit of that country's designation for T.P.S.

10. *How do I apply for T.P.S., once my country has been designated by the Attorney General?*
Here's what you need to submit to I.N.S.:
- Form I-765 Application for Employment Authorization (whether you wish work authorization or not, you must submit this Form; if you wish to get work authorization, you submit this Form with your check or money order to I.N.S. in the amount of $70);
- Form I-821 T.P.S. Eligibility Questionnaire;
- FD-258 Fingerprint chart (two samples);
- Two photos (¾ view, looking to left, right ear visible);
- Evidence of identity, citizenship, and residence in the U.S. for the required period (see next question).

11. *What is my required period of residence?*
When you first apply, there is no required period of residence: you may have just arrived in temporary stay status when the Attorney General designated your home country for T.P.S.

But if the Attorney General allows an extension, then you have to prove that you have been in continuous physical presence in the U.S. since that first designation.

This means that your departures from the U.S., if any, had to be brief, casual, and innocent, and did not meaningfully interrupt your physical presence (your unbroken day-to-day residence) in the U.S.

12. *How much of a fee do I have to pay I.N.S. to make my application for T.P.S.?*

The statute sets a ceiling for the T.P.S. application fee at $50. Unlike many other I.N.S. fees, which keep slowly rising, this one will stay right where it is.

13. *Once I apply for T.P.S., will I get work authorization?*

If you filed the Form 1-765 Application for Employment Authorization, and paid the $70 fee to I.N.S., you will get your work authorization when I.N.S. grants your T.P.S. application.

Be aware of the I.N.S. rule concerning filing the 1-765: it is filed at the local I.N.S. office along with a copy of the Form 1-821 application for T.P.S. status. You will pick up or receive by mail the Employment Authorization Document (E.A.D.).

14. *How long does my work authorization last?*

As long as the T.P.S. designation lasts, and as long as you are up to date in your filing of the necessary papers and payment of your fees.

15. *What happens to my temporary stay (nonimmigrant) status, once I apply for T.P.S.?*

It stays valid. It is not adversely affected by your application for T.P.S.

You are considered to be maintaining valid temporary stay status. This is a great boon if you become eligible to apply for adjustment of status on the basis of marriage to a legal resident, and if unbroken valid nonimmigrant status is a requirement, as it once was and might again become (see chapter 8 for discussion of the current adjustment rules, and a sketch of what the rules may be after October 1, 1997).

16. *I am a citizen of Bosnia, part of what used to be Yugoslavia before the break up of the country a few years ago. A terrible civil war has been raging there and still is. Am I protected by T.P.S.?*

Yes. On August 10, 1992 the Attorney General designated citizens of Bosnia-Herzegovina for T.P.S. protection for a one year period. That period has been extended each year since then, and is now extended until August 10, 1995.

17. *How do I prove that I am a citizen of Bosnia?*

Your Yugoslav passport shows your place of birth. That will be sufficient to prove that you are a citizen of Bosnia.

18. *My spouse, a legal resident of the U.S., filed a petition for me over two years ago. Will I have to go back to Yugoslavia for an interview before I get my visa?*

The new adjustment of status law, in effect from September 30, 1994 to September 30, 1997, takes care of that. You can stay right here and adjust status to legal resident.

Even before that law was passed, you had a safe visa interview alternative. You were considered homeless for visa interview purposes. As such, you were not required to return to Yugoslavia, and could instead have had your interview at the U.S. Consulate in Juarez, Mexico.

19. *Which countries in the world are presently designated for T.P.S. protection?*

There are only four as we go to press. If you are a citizen of one of them, you are covered by T.P.S. They are: Bosnia-Herzegovina, until August 10, 1996; Somalia, until September 17, 1996; Liberia, until March 28, 1996; Rwanda, until June 6, 1996.

If you are a citizen of one of these countries, check with any immigration lawyer as you are reading this book to see whether you are still covered by T.P.S.

20. *I am a citizen of El Salvador. I understand that I am no longer protected by T.P.S. Do I have any other kind of protection? I am still afraid to return to my home country.*

Let's give a little background to your question.

As a result of the belief of members of Congress that Salvadorans had been treated unfairly by the I.N.S. for years in the 1980s, the Immigration Act of 1990 provided a special Temporary Protected Status program for citizens of El Salvador.

When the program ended, a new status called Deferred Enforced Departure (D.E.D.) continued the rights of Salvadorans who had entered the U.S. by a certain date, to remain here and maintain work authorization. The program was good for the Salvadoran citizens involved, and it was good for their country's economy, which depended on moneys sent home to family members of Salvadorans residing in the U.S.

But the Deferred Enforced Departure program ended on December 31, 1994, as the U.S. government concluded that the political and human rights situation in El Salvador had sufficiently improved.

21. *What's going to happen to me, a citizen of El Salvador who had been on the Deferred Enforced Departure program?*

The I.N.S. will extend your work authorization for another nine months past December 31, 1994, until September 30, 1995.

You also have a right to submit or continue your application for asylum, and the I.N.S. is not expecting to press forward with those applications right away. You will probably have several years more before facing the prospect of deportation to your home country, assuming that you do not win your asylum application.

If you are a Salvadoran or Guatemalan citizen eligible for benefits under the so-called A.B.C. case (the American Baptist Church case), you will find special instructions for work authorization that supplement the Form I-765, and can get them by phoning 1-800-755-0777.

22. *Is there anything for me to do aside from applying for asylum?*

Maybe so. By the time I.N.S. decides your asylum case, you may have resided in the U.S. for seven years or more. I will assume that you crossed the border and entered the U.S. without inspection by an immigration officer, and that you were not paroled into the U.S. If you entered the U.S. seven or more years ago, and if you have no criminal record, you may well be eligible for something called suspension of deportation, when your case eventually comes before an immigration judge (see chapter 18, Question 8 for the parolee's ineligibility for suspension of deportation).

Of course, depending on your marital status, you may have the option of adjustment of status on the basis of a petition filed for you by a U.S. citizen or legal resident spouse.

The Visa Lottery

In writing the Immigration Act of 1990, Congress decided that citizens of certain countries in the world had not been receiving a fair portion of permanent stay (immigrant) visas to enter the U.S. for permanent residence.

These countries were called underrepresented, and Congress came up with a visa lottery procedure that is intended to give citizens of those countries a chance to be better represented, and to obtain a permanent stay (immigrant) visa, or to adjust to legal resident status. The program is called the diversity visa program (DV-1), or, after its chief sponsor in the U.S. House of Representatives, Charles Schumer, the Schumer visa lottery.

It is not so simple as filling out

a form and waiting for good luck to strike. There are some complicated things that you need to know about the visa lottery.

---

1. *How many years will the visa lottery last?*

It started in 1994, after several years of what were called "transitional" lotteries, and will continue indefinitely, unless Congress changes its mind and decides to eliminate it. Warning: in March, 1995 Representative Lamar Smith stated his intention to submit a bill that would eliminate the visa lottery.

2. *Which countries are ineligible for the Schumer visa lottery?*

Here is the current list of ineligible countries: Canada, Dominican Republic, El Salvador, India, Jamaica, Korea, Mexico, People's Republic of China, Philippines, United Kingdom (but natives of Northern Ireland are eligible), and Vietnam.

3. *How many visas will be issued each year?*

The total number each year is 55,000. No country can be awarded more than 7% of the total, or 3,850.

4. *Will some regions of the world do better than others?*

Yes. Here's the allotment of visas for fiscal year 1995 (ending September 30), by region: Africa, 20,200; Asia, 6,837; Europe, 24,549; North America (Bahamas), 8; South America, Central American and the Caribbean, 2,589; Oceania, 817.

5. *When do I apply for the lottery?*

The time will be announced by I.N.S. each year. It will be for a period of several weeks, and applications must be received during the stated period (neither before nor after). The 1995 period ran from 12:01 A.M. January 31 to midnight March 1.

6. *Is there an I.N.S. form that I have to use?*

There is neither a form to use nor a fee to pay.

7. *How do I apply?*

You use two pieces of paper: the application page, and the envelope.

8. *What do I put on the application page?*

You neatly write, or type, the following information on a plain sheet of paper (such as the 8½ by 11 inch sheet of standard typing paper):
- Your name, in this order: last name, then first and middle names. Underline your last name. For example: <u>Washington</u>, George Joseph;
- Your date of birth, in this order: day, month, year. For example: 20 March 1966;
- Place of birth: not the exact address, but include city or town, county, province, country;

- If you have a spouse and/or unmarried children under age twenty-one, put down their names, dates and places of birth;
- Your current mailing address;
- Native country, if different from country of birth.

9. *What is the difference between "native country" and "country of birth"?*

You know which country is your country of birth. Your so-called "native country" can also be the country of your spouse's citizenship.

This could be very good news for you.

Let's suppose that you are a citizen by birth of the Philippines, a country not eligible for the visa lottery. And let's suppose that your spouse is a citizen by birth of France, a country eligible for the lottery. You can be "charged" to France, and you therefore can and should put down your "native country" as France on the face of the application envelope.

Your spouse, meanwhile (assuming that he is not yet in legal resident status), can go ahead and apply on his own. He has France as his native country, and he lists you as his spouse.

Your name is therefore on two applications , and you have doubled your chances of winning the lottery. Not a bad position to be in!

10. *What do I need to know about the envelope?*

You need to consider size, address, and (equally important) return address.

- Size: Instructions specify that it must be between 6 and 10 inches in length, and between 3½ and 4½ inches in width. An ordinary business envelope is about 9½ by 4 inches, so we suggest that you use that type of envelope.
- Address: Address your application to: DV-1 Program, National Visa Center, Portsmouth, NH, USA. The zip code in Portsmouth changes for you according to the region of the world of which you are a native: Asia NH 00210; South America NH 00211; Europe NH 00212; Africa NH 00213; Oceania NH 00214; North America NH 00215. Make sure to get this straight. Otherwise, your application will be side-tracked, and who can say when it will get to the proper office to have a chance to be a winner.
- Return address. Upper left corner of the envelope: Write or type the name of your "native country" (the eligible country in our example above, see Question 9: not the Philippines, but France); Below the country name, put down your name and mailing address. Warning: If you do not include this information on the envelope, you will be disqualified.

11. Should I mail my application by Express Mail?

No. Mail by ordinary first class mail. Do not use Certified or Registered Mail, Express Mail, or Federal Express. Warning: If you do, you will be disqualified.

If mailing in the U.S., use a first class stamp (32 cent stamp as we go to press; check for subsequent change, if any). Use ordinary air mail if you are outside the U.S.

12. *How many applications can I mail in?*

Just one. If you mail two, and if the Visa Center discovers that, you are disqualified.

This rule requires a bit of discussion. The Visa Center has admitted that it does not have the technology to track whether anyone has mailed in more than one application. It would only be if two applications were approved for the same applicant that the duplication would be discovered, and both applications would be rejected.

Some applicants have therefore decided to mail in more than one application, hoping that the multiple applications will improve their chances, but not be so numerous as to risk a double-acceptance and the resulting rejection.

Be aware that submitting more than one application is a risky game.

13. *So far, this sounds fine. Are there any obstacles I should know about?*

Yes. There are two. First, a requirement of a certain level of education or work experience; second, the unavailability of the waivers that were helpful for the transitional lotteries.

14. *What are the education and work experience requirements?*

You have to show that you have the equivalent of a U.S. high school education, or two years of full-time paid work experience. Proof of that education or work experience does not have to be submitted with the application, but must be shown at the time of the interview scheduled after you are notified that you have won the lottery.

15. *Did I need to have any training before working for two years?*

Yes. The work that you did for two years must have required at least two years of training to qualify for.

16. *Doesn't that limit the visa lottery to highly trained workers?*

Yes. And that is a serious limitation.

The two year training requirement will disqualify many worthy foreign citizens, such as domestic workers who care for U.S. children and families, restaurant workers, garment industry workers, and mechanics.

These jobs require little or no training, or the training they require is in the nature of "hands on" experience. These workers, therefore, cannot get a Schumer lottery visa.

17. *What are the waivers that I may need, but cannot get?*

If you are here as a J-1 student or scholar, and are a winner of the Schumer lottery, you cannot get a waiver of the two year foreign residence requirement, as you were able to under one of the transitional lotteries (refer back to chapter 3 for the J-1 foreign residence requirement). All that you can do is try for the hard-to-get waiver of that requirement that was in the law before Schumer came along.

Here's another non-waiver that could be bad news for applicants for the Schumer visa. The very fact that you are in the U.S. may indicate that you, at some earlier point, committed what the I.N.S. considers to be visa fraud. If you came here as a visitor and over-stayed your permitted six month stay, the Service can say that you committed fraud because you told the consular officer who issued the B-2 that you would stay for a short time and return home. You did not.

If you entered without inspection (crossed the border), that is even more troubling, since you deliberately violated the immigration laws from the beginning.

At the moment, we do not know whether I.N.S. will take a strict or flexible view of these questions. Do they have it in mind to grant, or to deny?

18. *What should I do about these obstacles?*

You should confer with a good immigration lawyer, if you may have an admissibility problem. It may be necessary to file an application for a waiver of excludability, Form I-601. And the Service may, by the time of your interview, have given us some guidance on how strict or flexible they will be about excludability issues.

19. *Do I have to return to my native country for an interview after I win the lottery, or can I stay in the U.S. and adjust status?*

You can stay right here and apply to adjust status. Refer ahead to chapter 8 to see how this works. Unless you are still in legal temporary stay (nonimmigrant) status, however, you will have a total fee of $780 (the standard $130 fee plus a "penalty" fee of $650), plus medical exam, fingerprints, and four photos. It's expensive, but it's well worth it!

20. *Have any countries or regions eligible for the lottery already used up their allotted number of visas?*

Yes. As we go to press, Poland has reached its limit of 3,850 visas for the current fiscal year, and North America has reached its limit of eight visas.

Helping Your Spouse Get a Green Card

This chapter and several following explain how a legal resident or U.S. citizen can help their spouse obtain legal residence (get a green card). This is one of the "tried and true" ways to help a foreign citizen become a legal resident of the U.S., but it is also more complicated than it used to be. There is a very severe penalty, first of all, for entering into a marriage that is fraudulent: undertaken for the purpose of evading the immigration laws. There is also the difficulty of petitioning for a spouse who has been placed under exclusion or deportation proceedings.

Chapter 9 will consider the new (since 1986) feature of conditional residence for your spouse, and will discuss how and when to remove the condition. Chapter 10 will look at a 1994 law that makes it possible for a battered spouse who has not been petitioned for to file a petition for herself. Chapter 11 will see whether a widow or widower who was never petitioned for may be able to file a petition for herself or himself and get a green card.

---

1. *Do I need to have any special kind of marriage before I can help my spouse toward a green card?*

If you were married in the U.S., your marriage had to be performed according to the laws of the state where you reside. A marriage in "City Hall" follows those laws, and is perfectly acceptable.

If you were married abroad, the marriage should either have been performed by the civil authorities of the foreign country, or, if performed by the religious authorities, be documented by the civil authorities. An exception to this civil documentation requirement will be made if the U.S. State Department tells us that the country in question does not provide civil documentation for a religious marriage

2. *What makes a bona fide marriage?*

Your marriage has to be what is called a good faith or bona fide marriage. This means that you and your spouse got married because you wish to start out on a life together. You cannot get married with the sole and exclusive purpose of getting your spouse a green card, and without any genuine intention to start a life together.

Of course, if the marriage is bona fide, there is absolutely nothing wrong with taking steps to help your spouse get a green card.

3. *If the I.N.S. finds out that my marriage is not in good faith, what happens then?*

The first thing that happens is that the petition that you filed for your spouse will be denied by the I.N.S.

The second thing that happens, or at least that might happen, is that the I.N.S. asks the U.S. Attorney's office in the district where you reside to investigate your case to see whether the government wants to start a criminal prosecution of both of you.

If you are tried in Federal court, and convicted of entering into a fraudulent marriage in order to get an immigration benefit for your spouse, the consequences are severe: both you and your foreign citizen spouse can be punished by a fine of up to $250,000 each, and prison terms of up to five years.

After serving his or her term, your spouse will be placed under deportation proceedings to force a return to the home country.

Moral of the story: do not enter into a fraudulent marriage!

If the I.N.S. denies your petition on the basis of its belief that the marriage is fraudulent, you will need to get yourself a good immigration lawyer and contest the decision.

If the U.S. Attorney's office starts a criminal proceeding against you, you will need to get yourself a good criminal defense lawyer who can work well with your immigration lawyer.

4. *I am a U.S. citizen, married to a foreign citizen who overstayed her temporary visa. Our marriage is in good faith. What do I do to help my wife get a green card?*

You should ask "What do we do?" because you both have to do something. Here is what it is.

You complete the Form 1-130 Petition for Alien Relative for your spouse. You get the form from your local I.N.S. office (check the U.S. Government pages of your telephone directory), or from the I.N.S. Forms Center in your region (your local office will provide the address). Better yet, get it by phoning the I.N.S. toll-free number: 1-800-755-0777.

You will file it in person at the local I.N.S. office, when the time comes, with your check or money order for $80 made out to "Immigration and Naturalization Service."

Your spouse completes Form 1-485 Application to Adjust Status for himself or herself, with Form 1-485 Supplement A (designed to discover whether the new higher fee for adjustment applies).

You will file your wife's adjustment application in person along with your 1-130 visa petition. Since you are a U.S. citizen and your wife is an overstay, the fee will be only $130, plus the costs of a medical examination, photos, and fingerprints.

5. *What is adjustment of status?*

It is the procedure by which a foreign citizen, your spouse in this case, who is already in the U.S., can stay right here and change (adjust) status to legal resident status (get a green card), without spending the time and money, and having the uncertainty, of traveling back to the home country and being interviewed at the U.S. Consulate there for an immigrant visa to enter the U.S.

6. *Which foreign citizens can apply for adjustment?*

Before October 1, 1994 there were strict ground rules for adjustment that were set aside by the new law that took effect on that date. But since the old ground rules will probably go back into effect as of October 1, 1997, I have to tell you about the old rules as well as the new ones. If you qualify under the old rules, your fee is $130 (see Question 4 for a good example).

If you do not qualify under the old rules, and qualify only because of the new law, you pay a so-called penalty fee of $650, plus the old fee of $130, for a total new fee of $780.

7. *Who can adjust status, and still pay the old lower fee to I.N.S.?*

You qualify to adjust and pay the old lower fee if:

- You entered in legal nonimmigrant (temporary stay) status, and are still in that status;
- You entered in legal nonimmigrant status, fell out of status, but are back in legal nonimmigrant status when you file your application;
- You entered in legal nonimmigrant status, fell out of status, but are married to, and petitioned for by, a U.S. citizen;
- You entered in legal nonimmigrant status, filed an application for asylum while in that status, and the application had not yet been determined at the time that you filed for adjustment;
- You entered in legal nonimmigrant status, and were granted T.P.S. status before filing for adjustment.

8. *Who has to pay the new high fee when they adjust status under the new law?*
You have to pay the high fee when you adjust under the new law if:

- You entered without inspection (crossed the border from Canada or Mexico);
- You entered in valid nonimmigrant status, but fell out of status, and are married to, and petitioned for by, a legal resident (not a U.S. citizen);
- You entered on the Visa Waiver Program.

9. *I am in one of those three penalty fee categories. But why am I being penalized and required to pay such a big fee?*
Keep this in mind: under the former law, you were not eligible to adjust at all, and were stuck with the burden of what is called visa processing.

The new law saves you the expense of a round-trip ticket to the home country and a $200 fee for the interview and the immigrant visa. It also saves you from the peril of a visa interview: if the consular officer does not issue the visa, there is nothing that you can do about it, and you will be marooned in your home country.

By contrast, if your application for adjustment is denied, you will, at least, still be here. And if I.N.S. places you under deportation proceedings, you can renew your adjustment application before the immigration judge. For all these reasons, the new higher fee seems quite reasonable, given the great advantage of remaining in the U.S. and getting your green card right here.

10. *Does every foreign citizen who was not eligible to adjust under the old law have to pay the new high fee?*
This gets rather technical, but there are several exceptions to the new high fee. It does not apply to you if:

- You are under age seventeen, or are the spouse or unmarried child under twenty-one of a foreign citizen legalized under the 1986 legalization law ("amnesty"), and you were that spouse or unmarried child as of May 5, 1988;
- You entered the U.S. before May 5, 1988, and resided in the U.S. as of that

date, and you applied for Family Unity benefits under the Immigration Act of 1990.

11. *How soon after I file my petition does my spouse apply for adjustment?*

Since you are a U.S. citizen, she is what is called an immediate relative, which means that an immigrant visa is immediately available to her. When you file your petition, your spouse files her application for adjustment at the same time.

12. *Aside from the spouse of a U.S. citizen, does anybody else get the benefit of being a so-called immediate relative?*

Yes. Other immediate relatives are the unmarried child under age twenty-one of a U.S. citizen, and the parent of a U.S. citizen (but the U.S. citizen son or daughter has to be at least twenty-one to file a petition for the parent).

13. *If I were a legal resident with a green card, not a U.S. citizen, and filed a petition for my spouse, would he or she be able to adjust status?*

Eventually, but not right away.

An immigrant visa is not immediately available to your spouse if the petition is by a legal resident, not a U.S. citizen.

Your petition may be approved within four to eight months by I.N.S., but your spouse then has to "get in line" behind many other foreign citizens who have been previously petitioned for by legal resident spouses.

The wait is now about three years before your spouse is able to adjust status (if the new law is still in effect then), or travel back home to be interviewed for an immigrant visa.

Remember: your spouse will not be eligible to pay the old lower fee unless he or she is in valid nonmmigrant status at the time of filing the adjustment application. Otherwise, the much higher fee must be paid.

14. *I have a green card. I have petitioned for my unmarried daughter, who is age nineteen. What happens if she turns twenty-one before it is time for her to have her immigrant visa interview back home, or her adjustment interview in the U.S.?*

As an unmarried daughter under age twenty-one she is in Preference 2A (for spouse and unmarried son/daughter under twenty-one of legal resident). The waiting time between filing and having an immigrant visa immediately available is about three years. But if she turns twenty-one, she drops down to Preference 2B (for unmarried son/daughter twenty-one or over of a legal resident). The waiting time between filing and having an immigrant visa immediately available will be about five years.

Warning: Things could get even worse. The influential Commission on Immigration Reform recommended in June, 1995 that Congress eliminate the 2B Preference category altogether.

15. *Getting back to me, a U.S. citizen, and my Form I-130 petition for my spouse. Do I have to include some documents along with the petition?*

Yes. Here is what they are:

- Proof of your U.S. citizenship. This would be a photocopy either of your birth certificate, if you were born in the U.S., or of your naturalization certificate, if you were born in a foreign country and became a U.S. citizen through the procedure called naturalization.
- Statement concerning photocopies of documents. I.N.S. now accepts photocopies of original documents, such as naturalization certificates, green cards (I.N.S. Form I-551), birth and marriage certificates. Make sure, however, that you write or type this I.N.S.-approved statement and enclose it with your petition:

    "Copies of documents submitted are exact photocopies of original documents and I understand that I may be required to submit original documents to an Immigration or Consular official at a later date." You must sign and date this statement. It does not have to be notarized.
- Marriage certificate. If you were married in the U.S., this will show your name and your spouse's name, and the place and date of the marriage. If you were married abroad, the certificate should show the same, but might have to be translated.
- Certificate of termination of any earlier marriage. If either you or your spouse were married before this marriage, you must submit a copy of the court order that terminated the prior marriage, with translation if necessary.
- Your spouse's birth certificate to show his or her identity. If this document or any other document submitted is not in English, it must be translated.
- Translator's statement. The translator need not be a professional, just someone who is competent to translate. This statement should be enclosed with the translation:

    "I, (name of translator), certify that I am competent to translate this document, and that the translation is true and accurate to the best of my abilities."

16. *Would this list of documents apply just as well if I were not a U.S. citizen, but a legal resident with a green card?*

Yes, except that you would not be proving U.S. citizenship, but legal residence. You do this by submitting a photocopy of your green card (Form I-551). You must copy both sides of the green card, since both sides include important identifying information.

17. *Aside from the Form I-130 petition and these documents, is there any other I.N.S. form that I must include with the petition for my spouse?*

Yes. You and your spouse must both fill out Form G-325A Biographic Information. The form includes information such as the names and places of birth and residence of your parents. It also asks, for each of you, residence and employment history for the past five years. The forms should be typed, since the information needs to penetrate down through three carbons and onto three duplicate forms.

You and your spouse must sign the forms that you have filled out (to insure good copies, use a ball-point pen and press hard). If your wife is still in her home country, you must still get the Form G-325A to him or her for completion and signature, and you must file it along with the Form I-130 petition. This holds true whether the petitioning spouse is a U.S. citizen or legal resident of the U.S.

18. *Does I.N.S. need to see photos of me and my spouse?*

Yes. One photo of each of you: color photo against white background, head and shoulders, ¾ view looking to left, right ear visible. You write (do not sign) your names on the backs of the photos with Number 2 pencil.

19. *Aside from the fee, are there other expenses connected with my spouse's application for adjustment?*

Yes. The expenses of photos, fingerprints, and the medical exam.

- Photos. Your spouse needs to get another four photos of the type that were needed to go with your Form I-130 petition (different districts have different rules, but to be on the safe side, get four more identical photos).
- Fingerprints. Your spouse needs to get two samples (to make sure that at least one can be read by the F.B.I. and is not smudged) of the FD-258 fingerprint chart. Four photos and two sets of prints will cost about $23-$25.
- Medical exam. Form I-693 Medical Examination of Aliens Seeking Adjustment of Status. Your spouse must have this exam with X-rays and the test for H.I.V. infection by a doctor on the I.N.S. list that will be handed to you when you file the I-130 Petition for Alien Relative, and I-485 Application to Adjust Status (X-rays will be waived if a woman applicant is pregnant).

Note: Some districts require that you hand them the exam report at the time that you file the adjustment application, not at the time of the interview. You should check to see what your district's rules are.

Call several doctors on the list to compare fees. You should be able to get a complete examination, including all tests (H.I.V., tuberculosis) for about $125.

20. *Do I need to file any other forms and documents with my spouse's Form I-485 Application to Adjust Status?*

Yes. There is a one page form that the Internal Revenue Service wants the I.N.S. to forward to them. It is the Form 9003 Additional Questions to be Completed by All Applicants for Permanent Residence in the United States.

It asks for your spouse's Social Security number, if any, and whether he or she has paid taxes during the past three years.

21. *How exactly do I file the petition for my spouse and my spouse's application for adjustment?*

First, you make photocopies of everything that you will be handing over to I.N.S. (with the exception, of course, of the medical exam report that the doctor placed in a sealed envelope).

Then, you file the papers. I.N.S. offices have a location for the filing of petitions and applications, and a cashier's window nearby. You first go to the cashier's window and pay the required fees and get a receipt.

You then see an immigration examiner and hand the petition and application to him or her. The examiner will check over the submissions to make sure that they are complete (that they include the necessary forms, plus photos and prints), and will write down on an I.N.S. form a time and place for your spouse's adjustment interview, which you, the petitioner spouse, must also attend.

With the present huge backlog caused by the new adjustment law, your interview may not be scheduled for nine to twelve months after the date of filing, although that waiting time varies from district to district.

22. *Can my spouse get permission to work while on that long waiting line?*

Yes. At the same time that she files for adjustment, she files the Form I-765 Application for Employment Authorization with payment of $70 to I.N.S. She writes (c)(9) at box 16 of the Form I-765, which indicates that the request for work authorization is based on having filed an adjustment application.

New I.N.S. rules require that the application, with photos and fingerprints, be filed at the local I.N.S. office. The Employment Authorization Document (E.A.D.) will be picked up there or mailed out to her, and will be valid for one year.

23. *If my spouse has a family emergency back home while on that long waiting line, can she get permission to depart from the U.S. and return here?*

Yes. As of April 29, 1995 the I.N.S. announced a new policy of granting advance parole to applicants held up on the long line created by the new adjustment rules. You file the Form I-131 Application for Travel Document with photos and payment to I.N.S. of $70. You submit a copy of your adjustment application with proof of payment, and write a cover letter explaining the need for a brief visit home. I.N.S. will schedule your appearance and will grant the request "at the counter" of the local office on its Form I-512, stating that parole is granted for humanitarian reasons, and that you must return by a certain date.

24. *Will my spouse's application for adjustment be decided at the interview?*

Yes, unless the examiner feels the need to see more evidence than you have presented, or has some doubt about the good faith of the marriage or some question of admissibility that needs more time and investigation to resolve.

But, in most cases, the examiner at the interview will decide the matter then and there.

25. *What will the examiner be concerned about?*

The first matter of concern is the good faith of your marriage. The examiner usually makes a judgment about this on the basis of a "sixth sense," guided by experience, and observation of how the two of you conduct yourselves during the interview.

The second matter of concern is whether your spouse is what is called admissible to the United States. The Form I-485 asks questions about prior criminal record and other matters that could render your spouse inadmissible. The examiner will ask your spouse to affirm the truth of the answers, and may ask some specific questions that are on the Form I-485.

The FD-258 fingerprint chart will be checked by the F.B.I., and the interviewer may have, by the time of interview, some evidence of criminal record or lack of it.

A potential ground of inadmissibility that is always asked about is what is called public charge: is it likely that your spouse, at some time in the future, will have to go on public cash assistance?

26. *How does my spouse persuade the examiner that she will not be a public charge?*

Your spouse should bring to the interview proof that he or she is employed, or bring a letter from an employer who plans to employ your spouse as soon as he or she attains legal resident status and is authorized to work. If your spouse cannot show any such document, you will have to submit an Affidavit of Support for your spouse, by using I.N.S. Form I-134, which also affirms that your income will be "deemed" part of your spouse's income, for the purpose of eligibility for public benefits, for three years. You will need to show proof of your own employment and financial resources, and should be ready to show copies of your recent tax returns.

27. *What if all goes well and the examiner finds that my spouse is admissible?*

Then your spouse is home free. The examiner will place a red-ink stamp in your spouse's foreign passport: "Processed for I-551 ... Employment Authorized." To allow for delays in making and mailing the actual plastic card, the stamp is now generally made valid for eighteen months from the date hand-written by I.N.S. below the stamp. Make sure that you do not change your address during the wait for your green card.

In the meantime, the stamp in the passport is as good as a green card. With that stamp, your spouse can reside permanently in the U.S., work here, and travel in and out of the U.S. by showing the foreign passport with the stamp in it upon reentering the United States.

While waiting for the plastic green card to arriv.., you and your spouse should not change your address! Or, if you do, visit your local U.S. Post Office, and make sure that it will forward ma.. .o your new address.

28. *What happens after October 1, 1997, when this special adjustment of status program ends?*

We don't know yet. If the program is continued, keep following the instructions that we have given you above.

If the law goes back to where it was before October 1, 1994, life gets more complicated.

You, the foreign citizen, will not be eligible to adjust status in the U.S. and will have to return to your home country for a visa interview, if you entered the U.S. without inspection (illegally crossed the border from Canada or Mexico).

Assuming that you entered legally with a temporary stay (nonimmigrant) visa, you will not be eligible to adjust status if your spouse who petitions for you is a legal resident, not a U.S. citizen, and you have failed to maintain valid nonimmigrant status.

This rule points up another advantage of being married to a U.S. citizen and being an immediate relative: if you did not maintain valid nonimmigrant status, "all is forgiven" and you can still adjust status. The only absolute bar, even if married to a U.S. citizen, is having entered without inspection. Then you can still be petitioned for, but must return to the home country (for several days, not months) for a visa interview.

Stay tuned as October 1, 1997 approaches: we will see whether I.N.S. wishes to extend the three year experiment, or go back to the old way of handling adjustment of status.

29. *This is my second marriage. I have my green card and I would like to file a petition for my present spouse and help her to legal residence. I obtained my legal residence about two years ago as a result of a petition filed for me by my first spouse. Will I have a problem filing the I-130 petition for my present spouse?*

Yes, you will. Two years have gone by since you got your green card on the basis of a petition filed by your first spouse. The law says that your new petition cannot be filed until five years have gone by from the time that you were granted your green card.

30. *Doesn't the law usually permit an exception to this kind of strict rule?*

Yes, and it does in this case. You can get around the five year restriction if you can persuade the I.N.S., by clear and convincing evidence, that your first marriage was bona fide, and not entered into with the purpose of evading the immigration laws (or if the marriage was ended by the death of your spouse).

31. *How do I prove the good faith of my first marriage by clear and convincing evidence?*

I.N.S. regulations tell you that you must present the following evidence to show that the first marriage was bona fide:

- Documentation showing joint ownership of property during the marriage;
- Lease showing joint tenancy of common residence (joint apartment lease);
- Documentation showing commingling of financial resources (joint bank account, joint tax return);
- Birth certificate of any children born to the first marriage.

Affidavits of third parties who can affirm the good faith of the first marriage. The persons signing the affidavits should say that they are prepared to testify before the immigration examiner, if required to (this is very rarely asked for by I.N.S., but the statement conveys seriousness and sincerity). You, as the former spouse, should submit your own affidavit in which you explain your good faith in the first marriage from beginning to end.

32. *I entered the U.S. illegally by crossing over from a bordering country. I.N.S. picked me up and placed me under deportation proceedings. I was released on bond, and traveled to meet up with my fiancee, who had preceded me to the U.S., and we got married. She got her green card as a result of the 1986 legalization program ("amnesty"). Can she go ahead and file a Form 1-130 petition for me?*

Yes, but only if you and your spouse persuade the I.N.S., by clear and convincing evidence, that your marriage is bona fide and not a scheme to short-cut and evade the immigration laws. Look back to the previous question to see what evidence you and your spouse must present to I.N.S. to have a successful petition.

33. *If my spouse's petition is approved, is that the end of my deportation proceedings?*

No, not at all. You are still under deportation proceedings, and the fact that you are married to a legal resident does not protect you from being deported to your home country.

What you hope for, however, is that you can keep your deportation case going for the roughly three years that it will take before an immigrant visa is available to you.

If you can delay that long, you can then make a motion to the immigration court, or to the superior body called the Board of Immigration Appeals, and ask that they give you thirty days of so-called voluntary departure to go back to the home country for an immigrant visa interview.

This is complicated, and you certainly need a good immigration lawyer to help you through it.

34. *I arrived at the port of entry with a fake passport and visa and was placed under exclusion proceedings. While awaiting my hearing one year from now, I met and married a legal resident, who would like to file a petition for me. Can she do that?*

Yes, but it's the same story with exclusion as with deportation proceedings: you have to show by clear and convincing evidence that your marriage is not a sham. Look back to Question 31 and follow those instructions.

In your case, however, you will have an additional problem. The foreign citizen in Question 31 entered the U.S. illegally by crossing the border without being inspected by I.N.S. You did something more serious: you used a fake document to try to enter the U.S. According to the immigration law, it is better to enter the country without any document at all, than to try to enter with a fraudulent document.

Your fake passport and visa will have a negative effect on your admissibility to the U.S. Your lawyer will have to be creative to get you over this hurdle, and it will not be easy. Look back to chapter 4, Question 22-23 for some ideas.

35. *I was petitioned for by my spouse, who has a green card, about two years ago. Will I.N.S. let me know when my priority date has been reached, so that I can file for adjustment of status?*

No. I.N.S. will not contact you. You have to keep track of when your priority date has been reached, and then go ahead and file your adjustment application with I.N.S.

You can get this information from any immigration lawyer or immigration services organization, which have the monthly visa availability charts issued by the Department of State. Or you can look up these visa charts in one of the weekly newspapers listed in the Appendix.

Removing Conditional Residence

The questions in this chapter are not asked by the U.S. citizen or legal resident who filed the petition for a foreign citizen spouse. We are now ready for questions by that foreign citizen spouse who was just adjusted to legal resident status, and who has a green card, but on a conditional basis.

The conditional green card, invented by the Marriage Fraud Amendments of 1986, brings up questions about how to remove the condition attached to it, and what to do if you have been divorced, or battered by your spouse. This chapter tells you what you need to do.

1. *I married a U.S. citizen and he filed a petition for me. The examiner who interviewed me and granted my adjustment application told me that my green card would be conditional. Why is that?*

Here is the rule on when a green card is conditional, and explains why yours is: if less than two years elapse between the date of the marriage and the date of adjustment (or the date that you are admitted to the U.S. with an immigrant visa), your legal residence is conditional.

For all practical purposes, this rule means that almost every petition filed by a U.S. citizen for a foreign citizen spouse will get that foreign citizen spouse a conditional green card.

This will be so unless the examiner has some unresolved questions about the good faith of the marriage or the admissibility of the foreign citizen, and needs time to investigate further. If, as a result of delays, more than two years elapse between the date of marriage and the date of adjustment, your green card will not be conditional.

2. *Is my conditional green card like a card issued without conditions in any way?*

Yes. You should know that a conditional green card is just like one granted without conditions in several important ways:

1. You can work at any job in the U.S. with your conditional green card
2. You can travel in and out of the U.S. with the conditional card
3. Since you got the card as a result of a petition filed for you by a U.S. citizen spouse, you only need to wait three years (not the usual five) after being adjusted before being able to file an application for naturalization.

In these three ways, the conditional card is just like the one issued without conditions.

3. *How is my conditional green card different from one issued without conditions?*

At a certain point, you have to do something to remove the condition.

If your marriage is on-going, you and your spouse must file a joint petition to remove the condition on your residency. The two of you must do this twenty-one to twenty-four months after you were adjusted to legal residence on a conditional basis.

This means that you must file: Form I-751 Petition to Remove the Conditions on Residency, with payment of $80 fee by check or money order to "Immigration and Naturalization Service."

With the petition you enclose a photocopy of both sides of your Form I-551 Alien Registration card (green card).

4. *If my marriage has been terminated by divorce, can I still remove the condition and hold onto my green card?*

Yes, you can. Submit a copy of the court order of divorce with the I-751 petition. You must prove that the marriage was entered into in good faith, and that it ended through no fault of yours. Refer back to the previous chapter, Question 28, to see what I.N.S. needs to see to be satisfied that the marriage was bona fide.

5. *I am still married but am being battered by my spouse and subjected to mental cruelty. Can I still remove the condition and hold onto my green card?*

Yes, you can. A spouse who is mistreating you is not going to file a joint petition with you to remove the condition on your green card. Your spouse, indeed, is probably threatening to turn you over to the I.N.S. and have you deported.

Your spouse will not get away with that. What you need to do is apply for a waiver of the requirement that you and your spouse jointly file the petition to remove the conditions on your residency. The basis for your waiver request is the mistreatment that you are undergoing, and you can file for the waiver right away: you don't have to wait until twenty-one to twenty-four months after you got your green card. File for the waiver right now!

Here are the documents that I.N.S. needs to see in support of your application for a waiver (you use the Form 1-751 Petition to Remove the Conditions on Residency).

For evidence of physical abuse: submit reports and affidavits from police, judges (order of protection), medical personnel, school officials (if your child has been beaten and the school made note of it), social service agency personnel.

For evidence of mental cruelty: submit reports and affidavits from licensed clinical social workers, psychologists, psychiatrists.

6. *What are the different grounds for a waiver request?*

There are three (in addition to the obvious one that your spouse has died): you entered the marriage in good faith, but it ended in divorce through no fault of yours; you are still married, but being battered or subjected to mental cruelty; your deportation would result in extreme hardship to you.

7. *How do I prove extreme hardship if I am deported?*

Take a look back at chapter 3, Question 41, for a discussion of how to show exceptional hardship to get a waiver of what is called the two year foreign residence requirement of the J-1 nonimmigrant visa. There is no distinction worth talking about between extreme hardship and exceptional hardship: they are both very difficult to show, and a good lawyer is needed to help you put your argument together.

8. *When did the reasons for the hardship waiver have to develop?*

Here's a potential problem for you: the hardship has to develop during the period (which may be rather brief) of your conditional legal residence in the U.S.

9. *Am I limited to just one ground for my waiver request?*

No. But this requires some explanation. Form 1-751 asks you to "check one" basis for your waiver request. But the Board of Immigration Appeals, which reviews denials of waiver requests by I.N.S., tells us that you cannot introduce a second or third ground on your appeal, but must instead start all over again and file a new request with I.N.S. This suggests that, if more than one ground exists at the time of your application for the waiver, you should name all the grounds that apply, and provide evidence to back them up.

But your predicament of danger and anxiety cries out for the assistance of a good immigration lawyer who can appreciate what you have been going through, and can help you build the strongest possible case. Given the mistreatment that you have been subjected to by your spouse, it would be outrageous if you could not get a waiver of the requirement of joint filing, and hold onto your green card. Your lawyer will make sure that your battering spouse does not have the last word.

10

If You Are Battered

In 1994, a bill called the Violence Against Women Act became part of the Crime Bill passed by Congress and signed into law by the President. This new law makes it possible, although certainly not easy, for a battered spouse who has never been petitioned for by a U.S. citizen or legal resident spouse to "self-petition": to file a petition for herself, and possibly be awarded a green card. This surprising and, in our view, enlightened piece of legislation should be studied hard by any foreign citizen, not petitioned for by her spouse, who has had the ill fortune to be battered.

1. *I married a U.S. citizen three years ago. He told me he would file a petition to help me get a green card, but then he got mad at me and never filed the petition. Now things are going from bad to worse. I am being beaten by my husband, and he is threatening to turn me over to the I.N.S. for deportation. Do I have any hope of ever getting a green card?*

Yes, you do. The Crime Bill enacted in 1994 contains a provision that makes it possible for you to file a petition for a green card by yourself.

2. *How do I qualify to file a petition for myself as a battered spouse?*

You have to prove several things, some of them quite difficult:

- That you are married either to a U.S. citizen or to a legal resident (green card holder). You meet that requirement, since you are married to a U.S. citizen.
- That you are residing with your spouse, or at least resided with him before the battering began. From what you have said, you meet that requirement.
- That your marriage was a good faith marriage at its start. You should look back to chapter 8, Question 28, to see what kinds of documents you need to submit to prove that.
- That you are a person of what is called good moral character (for example, you have not lied to the I.N.S. to get an immigration benefit, and have not committed a serious crime). I will assume that you can meet this test.
- That you have been physically battered or subjected to extreme mental cruelty. Check back to chapter 9, Question 5, to see which documents you need to prove this. Given the difficulty of documenting mental cruelty, I.N.S. may show some flexibility here, and give you the benefit of the doubt.
- That your deportation or that of your child would cause you or your child extreme hardship. Check back to chapter 3, Question 41, for the difficulties of proving that.

3. *When the battering began, and went on and on, I insisted on a divorce, and my husband finally gave me one. Does that mean that there is no way that I can file a petition for myself now?*

All I can tell you about this is that the I.N.S. will not reject your petition for yourself solely on the ground that your marriage has ended.

If you can paint a dramatic picture of the good faith of your part of the marriage, the cruelty of your treatment by your former husband, and the extreme hardship that deportation would cause you, I.N.S. could grant you a green card in spite of the fact that your abusive husband is now out of the picture.

4. *What is the I.N.S. form that I use for self-petitioning, and what is the fee?*

As we go to press, there are not yet any formal I.N.S. regulations. However, a cable issued by the I.N.S. central office to the district offices in March, 1995 gave some useful information. You will use Form 1-360 Petition for Amerasian,

Widow(er), or Special Immigrant, with payment of $80. Where the box on Part 2 now refers to "special immigrant juvenile," you cross that out and write, as appropriate, "Crime Bill—Spouse of Citizen," or "Crime Bill—Spouse of Permanent Resident," or "Crime Bill—Child of Citizen," or "Crime Bill—Child of Permanent Resident."

You need to submit proof of the U.S. citizen or legal resident status of the abuser spouse, and that may require some ingenuity on your part. Indeed, it would be a good idea to get that information by copying the birth certificate or naturalization certificate, or green card, of your husband before the relationship has entirely degenerated, and your spouse will try to keep you from getting that information.

Your major task, after that, will be to submit evidence showing the abuse, the hardship to you if deported, and the evidence of your good moral character. This is a matter of vital importance, and you should not try to do it by yourself. Get a good immigration lawyer to help you along this difficult road.

11

If You Are a Widow or Widower

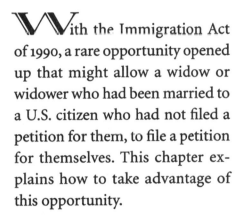

With the Immigration Act of 1990, a rare opportunity opened up that might allow a widow or widower who had been married to a U.S. citizen who had not filed a petition for them, to file a petition for themselves. This chapter explains how to take advantage of this opportunity.

---

1. *I married a legal resident four years ago. He never got around to filing a petition for me. He died last month. Can I file a petition for myself?*

No, you cannot. The law does not allow the widow or widower of a legal resident to file a petition for herself or himself.

2. *I married a U.S. citizen four years ago. He never got around to filing a petition for me. He died last month. Can I file a petition for myself?*

Yes, you can, if you meet certain requirements.

3. *What do I have to prove?*

Three things:

- That your spouse was a U.S. citizen (submit copy of marriage certificate, and of spouse's birth or naturalization certificate);
- That you were married for at least two years at the time of your spouse's death (submit copy of death certificate which, when compared to marriage certificate, will show length of marriage before spouse's death);
- That you have not remarried since your spouse's death (a suggestion: whatever marriage plans you presently have might be postponed for a while).

4. *Did my spouse have to be a U.S. citizen for the entire two years or more that we were married?*

No. It is only required that he was a U.S. citizen at the time of his death.

5. *How quickly do I have to file for myself as a widow or widower of a U.S. citizen spouse?*

You have to file your petition no later than two years after your spouse's date of death.

6. *How quickly will my petition for myself be approved?*

As the widow or widower of a U.S. citizen, you are in the favored category called immediate relative. Your petition for yourself should be approved within four to eight months of the date of filing, just as if your spouse were still alive and filing for you.

7. *Which form do I file, and what fee do I pay?*

You use Form 1-360 Petition for Amerasian, Widow(er), or Special Immigrant, with $80 fee to "Immigration and Naturalization Service."

8. *What happens to my children? Do they get the benefit of the petition for myself?*

Your foreign-born children will, like you, be considered as immediate relatives and be admitted or adjusted to legal residence, but must file their own Form 1-360 petition. They should do this, if possible, at the same time that you file your petition. If they file later, they have to go through the proof that you had to go through to prove your eligibility.

Your child's petition must also prove that you and the child had the appropriate parent-child relationships (check forward to chapter 12 to see what needs to be shown).

12

Helping Your Child Get a Green Card

A hallmark of the immigration law is family reunification. Congress has usually affirmed the importance of enabling legal residents and U.S. citizens to help their children back home, so that very close family members can end up living together in legal status in the United States. This chapter discusses how you, a legal resident or U.S. citizen, can help your foreign citizen children get to be legal residents of the United States.

1. *I am a legal resident with a green card. Which of my close relatives can I file a petition for and help get a green card?*

You can file a petition for your spouse, and for your unmarried child. If your child is under twenty-one, the petition moves slowly. If he or she is twenty-one or over, it moves much more slowly.

If you are filing a petition for a spouse or unmarried child under age twenty-one, you can expect to wait about three years before an immigrant visa is available for your relative, so that he or she can either adjust status (if in the U.S.), or get an immigrant visa in the home country and then enter the U.S. legally.

If you are filing a petition for an unmarried child who is twenty-one or over, you can expect to wait about five years before that relative is ready to adjust status or enter the U.S. with an immigrant visa.

Please note: as a legal resident, you cannot file a petition for a married child of any age, or for a parent.

2. *I am a U.S. citizen. Which of my close relatives can I file a petition for and help get a green card?*

We have already seen, in chapter 8, that you can file a petition for your spouse. That petition moves smoothly, since an immigrant visa is immediately available for your spouse. He or she can adjust status fairly soon, or, if still in the home country, will be able fairly soon to get an immigrant visa and enter the U.S. legally.

Your spouse is called an immediate relative. So is your unmarried child under age twenty-one, and your parent (so long as you yourself are at least twenty-one). For all your immediate relatives, an immigrant visa is immediately available, and they are on a moderately smooth track to a green card (it will still take some months to get there).

Moving somewhat more slowly would be your unmarried child age twenty-one or over, and your married child of any age. Moving very slowly towards a green card (it will take more than ten years, and as long a twenty) would be your brother or sister, and you have to be at least twenty-one to file a petition for them. It is hardly worth it: Congress, in fact, is considering abolishing the eligibility of siblings to be petitioned for.

Warning: The rules on the legal immigration of close relatives may change dramatically in the near future. The influential Commission on Immigration Reform has recommended that Congress restrict immigration to immediate relatives (the spouses, children unmarried and under twenty-one, and parents of U.S. citizens), and the spouses and children (unmarried and under twenty-one) of legal residents (the Preference 2A). This would have a devastating effect on the hopes for family reunification of a great many foreign citizens who are close relatives of U.S. citizens and legal residents.

The questions that follow, up to Question 11, assume that the questioner is in legal immigration status, either as a legal resident (green card holder) or U.S. citizen.

Questions 11-17 deal with U.S. citizen petitioners only.

3. *My wife and I were married in the home country, and she gave birth to our child there. We had to leave him there with his grandmother when we came to the U.S. What do we do now to get him here and help him get a green card?*

Your child is what the law calls a *legitimate child.*

If his mother files the Form I-130 Petition for Alien Relative for him, with payment of $80 to I.N.S., she submits:

- Copy of both sides of her green card if a legal resident, or of her birth or naturalization certificate, if a U.S. citizen;
- Copy of birth certificate of the child, with translation if necessary, showing mother's name.

The mother's name on the child's birth certificate should be the same as her name on the petition. If it is not, I.N.S. needs to see an explanation of the name change.

If you, the father, file the Form I-130 petition for your child, you submit:

- Copy of green card if legal resident, or birth or naturalization certificate if U.S. citizen;
- Copy of birth certificate of the child, with translation if necessary, showing your name as father.

Your name on the child's birth certificate should be the same as your name on the petition. If it is not, I.N.S. needs to see an explanation of the name change. Copy of your marriage certificate, and proof of the termination of any earlier marriage.

4. *My girlfriend and I had a love affair in the home country, and she gave birth to our child. We got married a year later. How do I help my child come to the U.S. and get a green card?*

The law calls your child a *legitimated child.*

Let's give a little background on how a child becomes legitimated, and when that has to happen. Warning: Make a note of these dates. They are very important.

A child can be legitimated as a result of:

- The marriage of the natural parents. Note: This marriage must take place before the child turns eighteen years of age.
- The law of the country of the child's permanent residence. Note: The law must take effect before the child turns eighteen.

The law of the country of the father's permanent residence. Note: The father must have resided there with the child while the child was under eighteen.

Documents that you submit:

- Copy of green card if legal resident, or birth or naturalization certificate if U.S. citizen;
- Birth certificate of your child, with translation if necessary;
- Parent's marriage certificate, or proof of law change that had the effect of legitimating your child (check to make sure that marriage or law change, when compared with birth certificate, shows that the marriage or law change occurred before the child turned eighteen).

5. *My girlfriend and I had a love affair in the home country, and she gave birth to our child. She then left the child and I don't know where she is now. The child is be-*

ing cared for by my mother. How do I help my child come to the U.S. and get a green card?

The law refers to your child as an *illegitimate child.*

For you, the father, to be successful in your petition for your child, you must show that you have or had a parent-child relationship while your child was under the age of twenty-one.

Before we discuss how to show that parent-child relationship, let's check to see whether your home country is one that has eliminated all distinctions between legitimate and illegitimate children, either before your child's birth, or before your child turned eighteen. If the law was passed after your child's birth it had to be retrospective, which means that it must cover those who were born before the law went into effect. If your home country has eliminated all distinctions I.N.S. will treat your child as legitimate, and you will not have to meet the burden of proving a parent-child relationship.

The countries that have eliminated the distinction between legitimate and illegitimate children are: Bolivia, Cuba, Ecuador, Guatemala, Haiti, Honduras, Trinidad & Tobago, and Yugoslavia.

Let's assume that your home country is not one of these, and that you have to prove a parent-child relationship.

First, you submit the Form 1-130 petition with the usual documents:

- Copy of green card if legal resident, or birth or naturalization certificate if U.S. citizen;
- Birth certificate of your child, showing your name as father, with translation if necessary.

If your name on the birth certificate differs from your name on the petition, I.N.S. needs to see an explanation of the name change.

6. *How do I prove a parent-child relationship?*

Here comes the challenging part. Proving a genuine parent-child relationship will be difficult if, as in your case, you left your home country when your child was an infant, and have not returned to visit, or have visited only a few times, leaving the job of caring for him or her to your mother.

Difficult, but not impossible. You must show, through documents and affidavits, that you have a genuine concern and interest in your child's support, instruction, and general welfare. You should show both emotional and financial support.

I.N.S. likes to see proof of on-going financial assistance through documents like money order receipts or cancelled checks. Note: Since these have been made out to your mother, not your child, you should get a notarized affidavit from your mother describing the amount and frequency of your financial contributions to your child's welfare, and stating how important to your child those contributions have been.

I.N.S. regulations mention other documentary proof of a father's help, but they

are relevant only to a situation where the father and child are already in the U.S. They include:
- Copies of the father's income tax returns showing the child as a dependent;
- Copies of the father's medical insurance policy, showing that the child is covered.

It would be a persuasive proof of concern if you have copies of letters that you wrote to your child's teachers expressing your concern about his or her progress at school, and letters you received from them (whether your child is in the U.S., or still, as in your case, back in the home country).

It would be important to submit letters between you and your child, if he or she is old enough to write to you. These letters will express your love for one another, and the hope that you will soon be united as a family in the United States.

I.N.S. will also consider notarized affidavits from friends, neighbors, school officials, or others who have personal knowledge of the caring relationship that you have with your child.

7. *I have just married a foreign citizen who has a daughter who is seventeen years old. That makes me her stepfather. Can I file a petition for her and help her get a green card?*

Yes, you can, and I am very glad to hear that you married your stepdaughter's mother when the girl was under eighteen years of age (check back to the Preface for a case where a petition was filed, and improperly approved by I.N.S., by a stepfather whose marriage to the mother took place when the young woman had reached eighteen, and the disastrous consequences of that error).

Make sure that you understand this rule very well: the marriage that creates the stepparent-stepchild relationship must take place before the child turns eighteen years of age. If she is eighteen or above at the time of the marriage, you cannot file a petition for her as her stepfather.

Documents to submit:
- Copy of green card if a legal resident, or birth or naturalization certificate if a U.S. citizen;
- Birth certificate of your stepchild, showing the name of the parent to whom you are now married, and translation if necessary;
- Your marriage certificate, showing (when compared to the stepchild's birth certificate), that the marriage creating the stepparent-stepchild relationship occurred before the stepchild turned eighteen years of age;
- Evidence of the termination of any earlier marriage of either party to this marriage.

8. *I have just married a foreign citizen who has a child who is seventeen years old. I would like to adopt the child, and file a petition for her. Can I do that?*

No. You are too late. Here's the rule: you had to adopt that child before she turned sixteen years of age, if you want to petition for an adopted child.

In your case, all is not lost. You are, after all, a stepparent, and you may petition as such, since the marriage took place when the child was under eighteen. File your petition as a stepparent, and look back to the previous question for details.

If you did adopt before the child reached age sixteen, you would submit:

- Your green card if a legal resident, or birth or naturalization certificate if a U.S. citizen;
- Adoption decree issued by the civil (not religious) authorities;
- Your adopted child's birth certificate, which, when compared with the adoption decree, shows that the child was adopted before reaching age sixteen;
- Proof that your child has been in your legal custody and has resided with you for at least two years.

Definition of legal custody: legal custody means the assumption of responsibility for a minor by an adult under the laws of the state and under the order or approval of a court of law or other government entity .

9. *I was granted legal custody by the court one year before I actually adopted my child. Does that year count toward the requirement that I show a two year period of custody and residence with my child before filing a petition for him?*

Yes, it does. The time that you had legal custody before you adopted the child counts towards the two years of custody and residence that you have to show before you file a petition for your adopted child.

If you did not have legal custody before the adoption decree, the two year clock starts ticking with the date of the decree.

10. *How do I prove to I.N.S. that the child has resided with me for two years?*

I.N.S. wants to see evidence that you own or rent the space that you and the child have been sharing. You need to show that you support your child and provide day to day supervision. You may use affidavits from persons of good reputation who affirm that you and your child have been residing together.

The Service needs to know details of the living arrangements, and be satisfied that the child is no longer residing with the natural parent.

After your adoption of your child, the child, in the future, will be unable to confer any immigration benefit upon her natural parent.

11. *I am a U.S. citizen. I am interested in adopting an orphan child in a foreign country. How do I go about it, and how do I file a petition to help my child get a green card?*

I am glad to hear that you are a US. citizen. Only a U.S. citizen can adopt an orphan child.

I also want to tell you right off that you must not only adopt that orphan child when he or she is under age sixteen, but also file a petition while the child is still under sixteen.

Avoid the tragic disappointment of successfully adopting a child who is under sixteen, but failing to file a petition until the child reaches the age of sixteen. That petition cannot be approved.

12. *Who is an orphan, according to the immigration law?*

An orphan is a child under age sixteen at the time that a petition is filed for him or her by a U.S. citizen, and who is an orphan either because of:

- The death of both parents;
- The disappearance of both parents;
- The abandonment or desertion of both parents;
- Separation or loss from both parents, or
- For whom the sole or surviving parent is incapable of providing the proper care, and has in writing irrevocably released the child for emigration and adoption.

If the orphan child was adopted abroad, it must have been adopted either by a U.S. citizen and spouse, or, if by a single U.S. citizen, that single citizen must have been at least twenty-five years of age.

13. *What qualifications should the parent or parents adopting an orphan have?*

The adopting parent or parents must satisfy the preadoption requirements of the home country.

I.N.S. must be fully satisfied that the child will be provided with proper care by the adopting parent or parents.

As in the case of non-orphan adoptions, the adopted child will not be able to confer, in the future, any immigration benefit upon the parent or parents who gave him up for adoption.

14. *What do I do if my wife and I have located the particular child whom we wish to adopt in the foreign country?*

You file with I.N.S. Form 1-600, Petition to Classify Orphan as Immediate Relative, with payment of $155 fee to "Immigration and Naturalization Service."

You include a copy of your birth or naturalization certificate to establish your U.S. citizenship (and, if you are a single parent, that you are at least twenty-five years of age).

The Service will decide all aspects of your petition:

- Your suitability as parents;
- Your compliance with any state preadoption requirements (if you will be adopting your child after he enters the U.S.);
- Whether your child fits the definition of orphan.

15. *What if we are going abroad in order to locate an orphan child for adoption?*

Here's what you do: You file with I.N.S. Form 1-600A Application for Advance Processing of Orphan Petition, with payment of $155 fee to "Immigration and Naturalization Service."

You include a copy of your birth or naturalization certificate to prove citizenship (and, if a single parent, that you are age twenty-five or over).

I.N.S. will evaluate your suitability as adoptive parents in the same manner as if you had filed Form 1-600. The Service will, if requested, forward the approved Form 1-600A application to the appropriate consular office or overseas office of I.N.S.

Important Note: When your Form 1-600A application is approved, your work is not done. You must then, once you have located your child to be adopted, go ahead and file the petition, that is, the Form I-600, and that petition must be filed before the child turns sixteen years of age. Do not miss this deadline!

16. *The child whom we wish to adopt was born out of wedlock, but is from one of those countries that does not make a distinction between legitimate and illegitimate children, so that the child is regarded as legitimate by I.N.S. Does that mean that I cannot petition for her because we cannot locate the father, and cannot therefore get both parents to release the child for adoption and emigration?*

Fortunately, the answer is "No." You cannot file a petition for the child as an immediate relative, that is true, but I.N.S. will let the child go with you to the U.S. on the program called parole, and from there you can file the petition that will result in the eventual legal residence for the child.

17. *How do I get parole status for my child?*

Here's what you do:

- Show that your Form 1-600A Application for Advance Processing was approved and is still valid;
- Show that you filed the Form 1-600 Petition to Classify Orphan as an Immediate Relative, and that it was denied (because I.N.S. regarded the child as legitimate, and the father could not be found to release the child for adoption);
- Show that your ties to the child were created before September 30, 1994 (when the current parole policy was announced), and that the Forms 1-600A and 1-600 were filed before that date.

We can all be glad that I.N.S. figured out a way to resolve what had been a heart-breaking situation for U.S. parents who were waiting in vain for a release in writing from a foreign citizen parent who could not be located, and who had never acted as a parent to the out-of-wedlock child whom the law defined as legitimate.

13

Visa Processing

In this chapter we discuss the procedure by which a foreign citizen who is still in the home country may be interviewed at the U.S. Consulate there for an immigrant visa (visa for permanent stay), on the basis of a petition filed either by an employer or by a close relative in the U.S. who is a legal resident or U.S. citizen.

Before October 1, 1994, visa processing was required for foreign citizens who were in the U.S., but who were not eligible to adjust status here, either because they entered the U.S. without inspection (illegally crossed the border), or had been petitioned for by a legal resident spouse but had violated their temporary stay (nonimmigrant) status, usually by staying longer than permitted, or by working without permission. Now all of those foreign citizens, if they can remain here until an immigrant visa is immediately available to them, are then permitted to adjust to legal resident status.

As of October 1, 1997 the new adjustment program ends (unless it is extended), and we may go back to the rules in effect before October 1, 1994. This chapter will focus on the situation as it now stands, and will continue until October 1, 1997. For more information on adjustment, go back and look at chapter 8.

---

1. *I am in the U.S., and am getting close to having an immigrant visa immediately available and being able to adjust status here. But can I choose, if I want to, to go back home and have a visa interview there, since I would like to visit my family anyway?*

Yes, but it will bring you a disadvantage. If you depart from the U.S. in order to attend a visa interview, you will not be able to receive your visa for ninety days after your departure.

2. *Is there any exception to this new ninety day wait rule?*

Yes. If you are in valid temporary stay (nonimmigrant) status at the time you depart from the U.S., the ninety day wait rule will not apply to you.

3. *I am a U.S. citizen father and my daughter (unmarried and under twenty-one) is back in the home country. My petition for her was approved by I.N.S. What has to happen before she gets a visa and comes to join me here?*

When I.N.S. approved your petition, they sent you Form I-797 Notice of Action, noting that the Service would have no further role to play in the case. The approved petition is sent to the Immigrant Visa Transition Center, and you will hear from them as soon as the Consulate in the home country is ready to proceed.

4. *What happens next?*

Since an immigrant visa is immediately available to your daughter, you will after a time receive an envelope from the Consulate that is called Packet 3. It contains an application for an immigrant visa, to be completed and mailed back promptly to the Consulate. As her father, you will know much of the biographic information called for in the application. The Consulate wants to get that form as soon as possible.

As soon as you get the documents listed in the Packet 3, you contact the Consulate, tell them that your daughter is ready for the immigrant visa interview, and request the Packet 4 and the interview date.

5. *What are the documents that the Consulate wants me to get ready for my daughter?*

Your daughter will need to show the consular officer who interviews her that you are qualified to petition for her. Send her a certified copy of your naturalization certificate. Send also the original and a copy of the certificate of marriage between you and your spouse. Write a note to the consular officer asking for the return of all original documents after the interview, including your marriage certificate.

Your daughter will need a passport, and four photos (in addition to the photo in the passport). The Consulate requires a medical exam, and has its own list of approved doctors and medical labs. The H.I.V. test is now required, and we hope and pray that there is no problem in that respect (if your daughter were H.I.V.-positive, she could not be admitted to the United States). Expect to pay about $125 for the medical exam and blood tests. The visa interview will cost about $200, and the visa itself another $75.

6. *How would this be different if I had been a legal resident when I filed the petition, but became a naturalized citizen while waiting for an immigrant visa to become available to my daughter?*

Write the visa center immediately, enclosing a copy of your naturalization certificate. They will switch your daughter from the slow Preference 2A track to the faster immediate relative track, and you will soon receive the Packet 3.

7. *At the interview, will my daughter get a lot of questions about her admissibility?*

Yes. The forms that she fills out are much like the Form 1-485 adjustment application questions. Your daughter needs to truthfully state that he has not committed a crime of moral turpitude, is not a terrorist, drug addict or trafficker. There are a long line of boxes, and we hope that your daughter will be able to answer "No" to the question: "Do any of these apply to you?"

8. *If my daughter is a student and not employed, or if she makes very little money, am I, as her father, going to have to answer the public charge question?*

Very definitely. You will need to check the yearly Health and Human Services figures concerning the poverty threshold (see chapter 4, Question 21). You must try hard, with your Form 1-134 Affidavit of Support, to convince the consular officer that you can pull your daughter, when you count the other members of your family who are dependent on you for support, above the poverty threshold level. Assuming that your daughter is in good health, and not criminal, it is the public charge question that is the most frequent stumbling block during a visa interview.

Reminder: There is no waiver or exception to the public charge ground of exclusion.

9. *If my daughter gets a visa, how soon does she have to leave the home country and travel to the U.S.?*

The immigrant visa that she gets from the consular officer is valid for four months.

10. *What does it look like?*

It is not a stamp in her passport, like the temporary stay (nonimmigrant) visa. It is a typing paper-size sheet of paper (8½ by 11 inches), with her photo.

11. *What happens at the port of entry?*

Your daughter's visa, of course, does not guarantee that she will be admitted to the U.S. by the immigration officer who inspects her at the port of entry, and that advice is prominently written on the visa itself.

However, unless the State Department finds something adverse about her at the last minute, and communicates it to the I.N.S., the immigration officer at the port of entry will look at the visa and the photo it contains, make sure that your daughter is the person depicted in the photo, and will mark her passport with the stamp that says that she is being processed for permanent residence. Her green card arrives in the mail several months later.

14

How Employers Stay Legal

In this chapter we look at the world not from the point of view of the foreign citizen trying to get a job and obtain legal residence, but from the point of view of employers who want to get good workers but also want to stay out of trouble with the immigration law. Before the Immigration Reform and Control Act of 1986 (I.R.C.A.), they had a free hand: they could hire workers of their choice, and not worry about whether they were or were not authorized to work.

Now it's different. If employers knowingly hire persons who are not authorized to work, they lay themselves open to fines of $250 per violation for the first violation (this would amount to $2500 if ten unauthorized workers are involved), and the fines multiply as the violations continue. If there is a pattern and practice of violations, criminal penalties can follow the civil fines.

The questions and answers in this chapter are designed to warn employers of the mine fields they may be stepping into if they are not careful about their hirings and terminations.

---

1. *I am the head of a household, and we need to hire a full-time baby-sitter. We are looking at a wonderful foreign citizen who does not have papers that authorize her to work. Do we have anything to worry about if we hire her?*

Yes. The law does not make an exception for an employer who hires just one person, unless the employment of that person is only sporadic. If the employment is steady and predictable (once a week, five days a week), you are subject to the law.

It is probably the case that the I.N.S. enforcement machinery is so busy with employers of large numbers of workers that it is not a high priority for the agency to seek out employers of baby-sitters. Still, it will be a risk for you if you go ahead and employ the excellent baby-sitter who is not authorized to work legally. It's not likely to happen, but if someone has a grudge against you and reports your hire to the I.N.S., you could end up being fined, and the baby-sitter could land in deportation proceedings.

2. *I run a small factory, and I am always looking for good workers. Do I have to check for green cards when I do my interviews?*

No. You are not supposed to start off interviews asking to see green cards. Indeed, you should not, at first, ask to see any documentation. You should first do the interview, and decide whether you want to hire the worker. If you decide to make the hire, then you ask for certain documents.

3. *Can I first ask the applicant if she is in legal status?*

No. That's not the right question: there are people who are in temporary legal status, and who are not authorized to work at all, or who are not authorized to work full-time.

4. *Well, what is the right question to ask of a prospective employee?*

The right question to ask is this one: "Are you presently legally authorized to work full-time in the United States?"

That question will get you a relevant answer, and it is a permissible question: you cannot be accused of an immigration-related unfair employment practice by asking it.

5. *What are the documents that I ask to see?*

You must require that the prospective employee fill out Section 1 of the I-9 Employment Eligibility Verification Form. The employee must present documentation required by Section 1 covering identification and eligibility to work legally.

6. *Do I need to fill out the Form I-9 if I hired the worker years and years ago?*

If you hired the worker before the date of enactment of I.R.C.A. on November 7, 1986 the worker is referred to as a *grandfathered worker*, and can continue as your employee for as long as you and he or she like, without the need for the Form I-9.

Of course, if the worker quits or is dismissed, and then later rehired, you have to treat him or her as a new worker, and fill out the Form I-9.

7. *Suppose I hire someone to put a new roof on my warehouse. Do I fill out the Form I-9?*

No. If you hire someone to do a specific piece of work, subject only to your satisfaction with the results, that person is referred to as an independent contractor. You do not fill out the Form I-9.

8. *I am a housewife, and once in a while I need a helper who can pick up one of my kids at school. Do I fill out the Form I-9?*

No. You are not required to fill out the I-9 for the "once in a while" worker, hired sporadically or casually, and not regularly and predictably.

9. *I need to hire a typical full-time worker. How soon after the date of hire do I need to check these documents?*

You must examine the documents within three days of the date of hire. You must ensure that the documents presented appear to be genuine (you are not required to independently investigate, or ask I.N.S. to investigate, to confirm that they are genuine), and that they refer to the individual to be hired.

10. *What else do I need to do?*

You fill out and sign Section 2 of Form I-9, the Employer Review and Verification.

11. *What are the documents that workers have to show me?*

They can show either an original document that establishes both identity and employment eligibility, or one original document that establishes identity, and another that establishes authorization to work.

If some documents have an expiration date, you must note that date on Section 2 of Form I-9.

12. *I really prefer to check green cards. May I insist that my prospective employees show me their green cards or I won't hire them?*

No, you can't do that. Regulations make it clear that you cannot specify which of several documents your prospective employees may present.

13. *Which are the documents that will kill two birds with one stone, by proving both identity and eligibility to work?*

Here is the list (any one of these will suffice) contained in I.N.S. regulations:

- U.S. passport (expired or unexpired);
- Certificate of U.S. citizenship (Form N-560, N-561);
- Certificate of Naturalization (Form N-550, N-570);
- Unexpired foreign passport with unexpired I.N.S. stamp reading: "Processed for I-551 (green card). Temporary Evidence of Lawful Admission for permanent residence. Valid until (date). Employment Authorized," or with Form I-94 Arrival and Departure Record with unexpired employment authorized stamp;
- Unexpired Alien Registration Receipt card (green card), Form I-551, with photo;
- Unexpired Temporary Resident card (Form I-688);
- Unexpired Employment Authorization card (Form I-688A);
- Unexpired reentry permit (Form I-327);
- Unexpired E.A.D. (Employment Authorization Document, Form I-688B), with photo;

14. *What are the documents that can prove identity?*

If your employees are age sixteen or above, they present one of the following:

- State driver's license or I.D. card with photo;
- School I.D. with photo;
- Voter registration card;
- U.S. military card or draft record;
- I.D. card issued by federal, state, or local government agency;
- Military dependent's I.D. card;
- Native American tribal document;
- U.S. Coast Guard Merchant Mariner card;
- Driver's license issued by Canadian governmental authority.

If the prospective employee is under age eighteen and cannot present one of the I.D. documents listed above, they can present any one of the following:

- School record or report card;
- Clinic doctor or hospital record;
- Day care or nursery school record.

If your prospective employees are under age eighteen and cannot show the documents just noted, they must follow all of the steps below:

- Parent or guardian completes Section 1 of Form 1-9, and writes "minor under 18" at the place for the employee's signature;
- Parent or guardian completes the "Preparer/Translator certification" on the Form 1-9;
- Employer, in Section 2, writes "minor under age 18" in space after "Document Identification."

Persons who are over eighteen but handicapped, who are being placed into employment by a nonprofit organization, association, or as part of a rehabilitation program, may follow the procedures provided for persons under age eighteen, above. Where the words "minor under age 18" were written in that context, the words now used are "special placement." In addition to parent or guardian, a representative of the nonprofit organization may fill out and sign the Form 1-9.

15. *What are the documents that prove eligibility to work?*
Here's the I.N.S. list:
- Social Security number card, unless "Not valid for employment purposes" is printed on it;
- A certification of birth abroad (to a U.S. citizen parent) issued by the Department of State, either Form FS-545, or DS-1350;
- An original or certified copy of a birth certificate issued by a state, county, or municipal authority;
- Native American tribal document (will serve to prove both identity and eligibility to work);
- U.S. citizen I.D. card (Form 1-197);
- I.D. card for resident citizen (Form 1-179).

16. *As an employer who is under the I.N.S. gun to prove that I am not hiring an unauthorized employee, I would be a lot happier if I could ask for two or three documents for I.D., and two or three to prove eligibility to work. Can't I do that?*
No, you cannot. If you ask for more than the minimum that I.N.S. regulations require, you run the risk of engaging in an unlawful employment practice. For example, if a legal resident shows you a state driver's license for I.D., and a social security number card for work eligibility, that's enough. If you refuse to hire her unless she shows you more, she can file a complaint with the Office of Special Counsel, and get job reinstatement and back pay from you. See chapter 17 on job discrimination. Don't make that mistake.

17. *Can't Congress do something to make life easier for the employer? How about having a single card for everybody that would prove eligibility to work legally?*
There are proposals to move toward a single tamper-proof card for everybody. But opponents point both to the enormous expense of creating such a card and making it reliable, and also object strongly to anything that approaches the sort

of national identity card that Americans associate with the dictatorial regimes of our time.

Congressman Dick Armey, the House majority leader, has recently put it this way: "What some are calling a 'national computer registry' is just a euphemism for a national I.D. card. And any system in which Americans would be forced to possess such a card, for any reason, is an abomination and wholly at odds with the American tradition of individual freedom."

We can expect Congressional temperatures to run high on this subject, and there is no way to predict the outcome.

15

Can Your Employer Help You?

It is more difficult than it used to be for an employer to help a foreign citizen obtain legal residence. If you are presently in illegal status, it is just about impossible. This is because the Immigration Reform and Control Act of 1986 (I.R.C.A.) introduced employer sanctions. This law prohibits employers from hiring persons who are not authorized to work legally in the U.S.

The employer is required to check the documents of each prospective employee to verify identification and authorization to work (see chapter 14). If he or she does not make a document check, or goes on to employ a person who is not authorized to work, the employer will be subject to a fine, which could be multiplied if the violations continue.

The procedure that used to be customary before the employer sanctions law, in which the employer would file a labor certification with the U.S. Department of Labor for someone not yet entitled to work and later file a petition with I.N.S. for the green card, has been short-circuited by the employer sanctions law. If the labor certification application contains entries that show that the employee cannot work legally (for example, that he or she came for a temporary stay that has expired, or entered the U.S. without inspection by I.N.S.), the Department of Labor is now required to make that information known to I.N.S. With that information, the I.N.S. will be in a position to fine the employer and to place the foreign citizen under deportation proceedings.

Most of this chapter, therefore, will consist of questions posed by foreign citizens who are still in valid temporary status, and wish to convert that status to legal residence, or who are still abroad and are looking for a way to immigrate (come permanently) to the U.S.

As you read this chapter, be aware that you can't do any of this on your own: you need a good immigration lawyer who can represent your employer. It is the prospective employer, not you, who must persuade the U.S. Department of Labor, and then the I.N.S., that the employer needs you, that you are not taking a job from a U.S. worker, and that you qualify for the kind of visa that you are looking for.

------

1. *I won a bronze medal in figure skating at the recent Winter Olympics. I would like to come to the U.S. and practice my profession there. Can I do that?*

Yes. As a bronze medalist in the Olympics, you are in that tiny group of foreign citizens of extraordinary ability who can actually file a petition for themselves with the I.N.S., and look forward to the prospect of permanent residence and a green card. Actually, any person can file a petition for you, and that of course includes a prospective employer.

What it amounts to is this: Uncle Sam wants you! If you are in that very top level of accomplishment, your work will almost certainly be good for the U.S. economy and enhance our national prestige.

2. *Do I just send a copy of my Olympic award to I.N.S. and automatically get a green card?*

There's more to it than that. You have to demonstrate that the acclaim for your achievements has been sustained over a period of time (that you are not just a "flash in the pan").

To work your way to a bronze medal, you must have won competitions and awards leading up to that, and you should show evidence of those earlier signs of acclaim, a well as of the Olympic medal.

3. *Do I have to be world famous?*

As an Olympic medalist, you are world famous. However, to qualify for the extraordinary ability visa your sustained acclaim can be either national or international. In other words, you might well have qualified while you were still just the national champion, and before you went to the Olympics.

4. *How do I file my application?*

You file the Form 1-140 Immigrant Petition for Alien Worker, with payment of $75 to "Immigration and Naturalization Service."

5. *Where do I file my petition?*

You mail the petition to the I.N.S. Regional Center for the region where you will be employed (or, in your case, self-employed). The instruction pages to Form 1-140 will give you the addresses.

6. *Is this self-petitioning option available only to champion athletes?*

No. The extraordinary ability visa for legal residence is for a person who has that ability in any one of five fields of endeavor. The five, which you will remember from our discussion of nonimmigrant workers in chapter 3, Question 94, are: Sciences, Arts, Education, Business, and Athletics.

7. *What kind of evidence does I.N.S. need to see to be satisfied that I am extraordinary in one of the five categories?*

Whether you petition for yourself or are petitioned for by an employer, you need to present evidence of your receipt of prizes or awards and of the esteem that you are held in by your peers. Since the world generally backs up its evaluations by financial reward, it helps if you can show that your extraordinary accomplishment had been well rewarded in the marketplace.

If you are in the performing arts, I am sorry to say that the instructions do not say that critical appreciation alone is enough: I.N.S. wants to see commercial success, measured by such signs of success as box office receipts or record sales. The high quality performing artist who is critically acclaimed but commercially undervalued may have a tough time getting I.N.S. to see him or her as extraordinary.

8. *Aside from the extraordinary ability person, are there other highest level workers who are given a special exemption by the immigration law?*

Yes, there are. Let's first remind ourselves of what we mean by a special exemption. That means that the employer does not have to go through the trouble and delay of first filing what is called a labor certification application with the Department of Labor, and then waiting for something called the priority date to be reached before filing the Form 1-140 petition with I.N.S.

The other highest level workers who don't need labor certifications are *outstanding professors and researchers,* and *multinational managers and executives.*

Again, Congress evidently decided that the U.S. needs these workers in order to remain competitive in the so-called new global economy.

9. *How do I prove to I.N.S. that I am an outstanding professor?*

Put in extensive documentation of your teaching, service to the university, publications, and acclaim by peers in your field of specialization.

The job offer has to be for a so-called tenure-track position, which means that the expectation is that satisfactory performance will lead to a permanent, life-time position in the college or university. You must show that you have had at least three years of previous teaching experience as a professor in the field in which you are regarded as outstanding.

10. *What if the three years of teaching were done while I was working on an advanced degree?*

That would be acceptable if you actually got the advanced degree, and if you can show that you had full responsibility for the courses that you taught.

11. *Are the requirements any different if I am an outstanding researcher?*

The job does not have to be tenure-track, but it cannot have a fixed date of termination, and there should be an expectation that satisfactory performance will lead to a permanent position.

As with the teaching professor, you must show three years of previous experience doing high-level research.

12. *I worked as a manager for a big company in my home country last year. Can I get a visa as a manager and then look for a good manager's job in the U.S.?*

No, that's not how it works. You must have worked for one out of the last three years as a manager or executive. This you have done. But you must have worked as a manager for the same multinational company that intends to continue to employ you in the U.S., or to do so at its affiliate or subsidiary.

So, you have to stay with your company. You cannot jump ship and try to start working for a different multinational corporation, or you will not qualify for the multinational manager or executive visa.

13. *I worked for a year in the temporary stay (nonimmigrant) visa category called L-1 (manager or executive). Does that count as the one-out-of-three years as manager or executive that I have to show I.N.S.?*

Yes, it does. If you worked for one year in L-1 temporary stay (nonimmigrant) status, you may count that as the required one year out of the last three of employment as a manager or executive.

14. *When we put all of these highest level visas together, what are the numbers per year that we are talking about?*

When we put together all of these highest level visas that do not require a labor certification (the extraordinary ability persons in the five categories, the outstanding professors and researchers, and the multinational managers and executives), we are talking about 40,000 visas per year, including their spouse and child (unmarried son or daughter under age twenty-one).

15. *Does the law give a name to these highest level workers?*

They are called priority workers, and they are grouped in what is called the First Employment Preference.

16. *If I qualify for one of the First Preference visas, how long is my wait before I get it?*

You are on a fast track. The State Department publishes information monthly on all of the employment preference categories. The First Preference has been consistently current, which means that there is no waiting line to reach the visa. As soon as I.N.S. reviews and evaluates your employer's petition, it will be approved and your permanent resident visa will be issued.

17. *What if I do not qualify for one of those highest level visas. What's the next step down?*

The next step down is for foreign citizens who either have *advanced degrees* or their equivalents, or have *exceptional ability* in one of three categories: Sciences, Arts, or Business.

18. *What happened to Education and Athletics, that were part of the First Preference extraordinary ability visa?*

For some reason they are left out of this stepped-down category. If you are in those fields, have your lawyer try harder to persuade I.N.S. that you are truly extraordinary, and belong in First Preference.

19. *Does the law have a name for this stepped-down category?*

It is called Second Preference.

20. *How many visas per year are we talking about?*

As many as for the First Preference: 40,000 per year, including spouses and children (unmarried sons or daughters under age twenty-one).

21. *If I qualify for a Second Preference visa, how long will I need to wait for it?*

First, your employer will have to file the application for labor certification for you, and this can take a year or more before approval.

Once the Department of Labor approves, you will then be on a fast track, and your employer will in all likelihood be able to file the visa petition for you without waiting.

22. *Compared to the highest level visa category (First Preference), is there any disadvantage to being in this slightly lower category (Second Preference)?*

Yes. There are two hurdles that you have in Second Preference that you would not have if you qualified for First Preference.

First, your employer will have to file a labor certification application for you with the U.S. Department of Labor. Second, the law requires that your employer persuade I.N.S. that you will, after your admission, substantially benefit the U.S. national economy, cultural or educational interests, or welfare.

23. *How do we do that?*

Here's where your lawyer shows imagination and creativity.

It's partly just a matter of common sense. What kind of work do you do? How will it have a positive impact on the town or city where you will be working? What are the needs of the community in the U.S. where you will be residing, and how will you help to meet those needs?

The answers will depend on the specific plans and projects that you have, that we hope will strike the I.N.S. as making a positive contribution to the U.S. If you are an orchestra conductor, for example, will you spend at least a portion of your time visiting high schools, and giving their orchestras a sample rehearsal?

Your employer's petition should be supported by affidavits from people in the community who will be substantially benefited by your presence and activities.

24. *In connection with Second Preference workers with advanced degrees or their equivalents: what is the equivalent of an advanced degree?*

You will have the equivalent, and thus qualify for Second Preference, if you have the basic B.A. (Bachelor of Arts) or B.S. (Bachelor of Science) degree, plus five years of what is called progressive experience in the profession (where you are given more and more responsibility).

25. *I am negotiating for a position as a university teacher of chemistry. But I am told that I need the Ph.D. (Doctor of Philosophy) degree. I have the master's degree and five years of teaching. Is that the equivalent of the Ph.D.?*

No. It is not the equivalent, and you therefore do not qualify for Second Preference.

There is a special rule concerning the Ph.D. degree. If it is customarily required in your specialty, you must get that degree to be qualified as the Second Preference holder of an advanced degree. The master's degree and five, or even ten, years of experience would not be enough. Go ahead and get that Ph.D. degree!

26. *I have been doing high level research on A.I.D.S., and have been recognized as an authority in this field. Since this is important work, can I get a Second Preference visa without having a job offer right now?*

Yes, you probably can. A job offer and a labor certification are the usual requirements for someone looking for a Second Preference visa. But that requirement may be waived by the Attorney General (that is, by I.N.S.) if your admission to the U.S. with a visa would be in the national interest.

A national interest waiver must be based on something more than an economic benefit to the U.S. Given the crisis that is posed by A.I.D.S., you would be a good candidate for the national interest waiver. A solution to the A.I.D.S. crisis would be of enormous humanitarian, as well as economic, benefit to the United States.

27. *I have the advanced degree that will qualify me for Second Preference. But the best job offer that I have received so far is for a position as a high school teacher. Do I still qualify for Second Preference?*

No. You cannot qualify for Second Preference if the job offer does not require a person with an advanced degree or its equivalent.

You may try to argue that your work as a high school teacher would substantially benefit U.S. educational interests. But if the job offer does not require an advanced degree, you are not a candidate for Second Preference.

28. *Well, then, what am I qualified for?*

We need to drop down and look at the Third Employment Preference. This includes:

- *Professionals* (basic bachelor's degree, and a job that requires that degree);
- *Skilled workers* (with at least two years of training or experience);
- *Other workers* (with less than two years of training or experience).

You would qualify as a professional: you have the basic degree required (actually, you have a higher degree, but it can't do you any good), and your high school teaching job presumably requires the basic college degree.

29. *How many visas per year are allotted to these workers?*

The same as for First and Second Preference: 40,000 visas per year, including spouses and children (unmarried sons or daughters under age twenty-one).

However, the three categories are not evenly divided. Congress showed little concern for people with basic skills, including household domestic workers who care for the children, or elderly parents, of U.S. citizens. It therefore limited those so-called other workers to 10,000 visas per year.

30. *If I qualify for Third Preference, how much of a wait in line should I anticipate?*

In all three categories of Third Preference, your employer has to file a labor certification application, which can take a year or more before approval.

Assuming that the labor certification is approved, here's what happens with the different categories (this estimate is accurate as we go to press):
- Professionals: current, no waiting line, but processing time will take several months;
- Skilled workers: current, no waiting line, but processing time will take several months;
- Other workers: the waiting line is over 4½ years in length. For example, if your employer filed a labor certification for you in October, 1990, he or she could theoretically have filed a Form I-140 visa petition for you in June, 1995, about 4½ years later. However, the line moves about two weeks forward each month, which means that it could in fact take eight or nine years for the so-called other worker to get an immigrant visa leading to a green card.

Warning: The influential Commission on Immigration Reform recommended to Congress in June, 1995 that it eliminate the so-called other worker visa category altogether.

31. *I have always been interested in religion, and I was a long-time church member in my home country. Can I get a visa and go to work for a church in the U.S.?*

If that's the extent of your background, the answer is "No."

Ministers and religious workers are called special immigrants. They occupy the Fourth Employment Preference, and up to 10,000 of them per year (including spouses and children who are unmarried and under age twenty-one) may receive a visa.

The religious workers, as distinct from the ministers, are limited to a maximum of 5,000 visas per year.

You would have to prove that for at least two years before making your application for admission you had been a member of a religious denomination having a bona fide, nonprofit religious organization in the United States.

You also have to show that you intend to enter the U.S. solely for the purpose of carrying on work as a minister, or religious worker, for that same religious organization. In other words, you cannot use your two years of work in the home country as a springboard to leap into a different religious organization in the U.S.

32. *I heard that the minister visas were being continued, but that the religious worker visas were being phased out. Is that true?*

A phase out of the religious worker visas was set for October 1, 1994, but Congress stepped in and continued the program for three years until October 1, 1997.

33. *How do I, as a minister or religious worker, apply for a visa?*

You, or the organization that employs you, file with I.N.S. the Form I-360 Petition for Amerasian, Widow(er), or Special Immigrant, with payment of $80 fee to "Immigration and Naturalization Service."

34. *Can someone who is very rich "buy" a green card"*

No. But I know what you are thinking about. There is a new visa that came in with the Immigration Act of 1990, which is called the entrepreneur visa, and nicknamed "the millionaire's visa."

If someone is ready to invest a million dollars in an enterprise that will employ at least ten full-time U.S. workers (this category includes primarily U.S. citizens and legal residents), up to 10,000 per year of these entrepreneurs (including spouses and children) may receive a visa leading to legal residence. If the person is willing and ready to set up the enterprise in an area that is affected by a very high unemployment rate, the amount to be invested drops to a half million dollars.

This law has been on the books since 1990, and few millionaires or demimillionaires have shown much interest in it.

The entrepreneur occupies the Fifth Employment Preference.

35. *Is there a form to file and a fee to pay by the entrepreneur?*

The form to file is Form I-526 Immigrant Petition by Alien Entrepreneur, and the I.N.S. fee to pay is $155.

16

Labor Certification

Labor certification is the process by which an employer shows the state and U.S. Department of Labor that hiring the foreign citizen worker will not adversely affect the U.S. work force. It is an application that is filed by the employer, not by the foreign citizen, and it is the employer, with the help of an immigration lawyer, who prepares the papers and responds to requests for further proof from the Department of Labor.

Unless you, the foreign citizen, are in the highest level of so-called priority workers, you or your employer cannot go straight to the I.N.S. and file a petition. Your employer files an application first with the Department of Labor. After that application is approved, which may take a year or more, the employer files a petition with the I.N.S. to move you toward legal status and your green card.

It is a complicated process, and it requires the help of an immigration lawyer. You yourself cannot work it out with your employer, and you shouldn't try. Our brief discussion of labor certification, therefore, will be just an outline. It is very definitely not a substitute for the immigration attorney who is essential both to the employer and to you, the foreign citizen.

---

1. *Is there any way for me to avoid the labor certification process, and go straight to I.N.S. with a visa petition?*

If you are one of the highest level workers, your employer does not have to get you a labor certification. If you are on the next highest level, and I.N.S. is persuaded that it would be very much in the national interest for to be admitted to the U.S., you may be able to do without a job offer and a labor certification (refer back to chapter 15).

But for foreign citizens who are ordinary mortals, and not luminaries, your employer has to work through the labor certification process.

2. *If I entered without inspection and am not authorized to work by I.N.S., will my employer be able to get me a labor certification?*

Ten years ago, the answer would have been "Yes, if you qualify." Since 1986 and the introduction of the employer sanctions law, the answer is "No, unless your employer is willing to risk being fined for employing someone who is not authorized to work." And it is rare indeed to find an employer who would knowingly take that risk.

3. *Why does the Department of Labor and I.N.S. have to find out that I entered without inspection? Can't I just keep that quiet?*

Your employer has to submit the Form ETA 750A/B Application for Alien Employment Certification. The Part A Offer of Employment, Question 3, asks for your type of visa, if you are in the U.S. Your employer cannot truthfully say that you have a visa that permits work. And a false statement on this form could subject the employer to criminal prosecution.

If the employer truthfully puts down "E.W.I." (Entered Without Inspection), the Department of Labor is now required to communicate that information to the I.N.S. If this is done, and if the Service activates its enforcement machinery, your employer could be fined for hiring someone who is not entitled to work legally, and you could be placed under deportation proceedings.

4. *I applied for asylum and my case is pending. I have work authorization. Can my employer file a labor certification application for me?*

Yes. Under Part A, Question 3, your employer can write in the number of the Code of Federal Regulations that is written on your Employment Authorization Document (Form I-688B), which refers to your authorization to work.

Since an asylum case normally takes more than a year to conclude, and you will make sure to keep your work authorization current during that period, you will be authorized to work while your labor certification application is being processed.

5. *What does the Department of Labor need to know to grant the application for labor certification?*

That your employment will not take a job from a U.S. worker.

6. *Who is a U.S. worker?*

For our purposes, and I am simplifying a bit, a U.S. worker is either a U.S. citizen, a legal resident, or someone who has been granted asylum. These are the people whose rights to a job the Department of Labor is protecting.

7. *The Department of Labor is not just concerned about U.S. citizen workers?*

That's right. The Department of Labor is also concerned about the rights of foreign citizens who are entitled to work permanently in the U.S.

8. *How does my employer prove that I am not taking a job from a U.S. worker?*

The employer places an advertisement for the position in an appropriate newspaper, and also lists it with the local state Department of Labor, which makes the availability of the position known.

Here's the question that the Department of Labor is interested in: is there a U.S. worker who is qualified for the job, and available to take it at the time and place where it is offered? If there is such a U.S. worker, the labor certification application will be denied.

9. *Wait a minute. Won't I, as a foreign citizen, get a labor certification if I am better qualified than the U.S. worker?*

Not necessarily. The general rule is that he U.S. worker does not have to be as well qualified as the foreign worker, just minimally qualified for the job.

10. *Is there any exception to that general rule?*

Yes. There is a so-called special rule for certain foreign citizen workers. If you are a member of the teaching professions, or if you are a person of exceptional ability in the sciences or arts, the U.S. worker has to be more than just minimally qualified: they have to be every bit as good as you are. If they are only minimally qualified, you will merit the labor certification.

11. *Let's say that my employer and his or her lawyer succeed, and I am granted a labor certification. Does that mean that I am now legally authorized to work?*

No, it does not mean that. This may come as a shock to you, but a labor certification approval does not authorize you to work legally. You will be authorized to work only when your so-called priority date is reached, your lawyer files with I.N.S. the Form 1-140 Immigrant Petition for Alien Worker, and you are either admitted as an immigrant or your status is adjusted to legal residence.

Your priority date is set by the time that the Department of Labor receives your application (hence the importance of mailing it by certified mail, return receipt requested). Depending on how high-level or modest-level your work is, it may take hardly any time at all, or many years, for your priority date to be reached, so that your employer can file a petition with I.N.S.

12. *How do I get from being labor certified to being authorized to work legally?*

Your lawyer checks the State Department's monthly map of visa availability. When your priority date is reached, your employer files the Form 1-140 petition, with payment of the $75 fee to "Immigration and Naturalization Service." With it, you include a copy of the labor certification approval.

The I.N.S. makes its own independent determination of whether you qualify for the preference category that you are certified for.

13. *I have been working for a year as a baby-sitter and child care giver for an American family with two young children. Can my employer help me get a labor certification and then a green card?.*

There are two separate questions here: whether you can get a labor certification, and then whether you can wait long enough for your priority date to be reached, so that your employer can help you get a green card.

Let's first discuss the labor certification. To be eligible for labor certification as a baby-sitter and child care giver (the law calls you a *household domestic service worker*, which doesn't really do you justice) you have to show that you have already had one year of full-time paid work as a child care giver behind you. From what you have said, it looks like you can get over that threshold.

If your employer advertises for a child care giver, and offers a reasonably good salary, there is a good chance that a U.S. worker will respond to the ad, especially if we are still experiencing economic hard times in the U.S. We already know that the U.S. worker does not have to be as good as you are, or as well liked by your employer's children as you are. She only needs to be minimally qualified. If she is, you can't get a labor certification.

For this reason, it may be desirable for you to work as a live-in child care giver, if your employer wishes this, since it is harder to find a U.S. worker who is ready to live in. Assuming that you are ready and willing to live in, your employer will have to show the Labor Department that it is a so-called *business necessity* (we really mean a necessity for the proper running of the household) for the employer to hire someone who can live in. Your employer can do this if she and her husband work long and sometimes unpredictable hours, and one or both of them are often required to be out during evenings to attend to their professional lives. Under these circumstances, which the employer must prove by documentation and affidavits, the household would be in jeopardy unless you could live in and take care of the children when the parents cannot be at home. In such a case, your employer could meet the so-called business necessity test.

Needless to say, you can't win your case on your own. You, and your employer, need the help of a good immigration lawyer who knows the ins and outs of labor certification.

14. *If my employer and our lawyer succeed, and I am labor certified, how long a wait do I have before getting my green card?*

Now I have to give you some bad news. Since your job requires little training or experience (although it requires some very important personal qualities that the law has no way of measuring or of thanking you for), you are one of the so-called "other workers" who are entitled to only 10,000 visas per year.

The visa availability chart that the State Department publishes each month suggests that you may have between 4½ and 9 years to wait before your priority date is reached, and an immigrant visa is ready for you. Is the family going to need you for full-time live-in work between 4½ and 9 years from now, when the two children will be a lot older and less dependent? That is a big question. And you will not be granted a visa by the U.S. Consulate in your home country, or adjusted status in the U.S. by I.N.S., unless the conditions that were stated in the Labor Certification application remain the same at the time of your future interview.

Foreign citizens who are baby-sitters and child care givers are perhaps doing more for American families than any other foreign citizen worker, including the high-tech workers who are helping us to compete in the global marketplace. But the immigration law is not doing much for you, and you can work for many years for an American family, and may never get an immigration benefit at the end of the road on the basis of that vitally important work.

There is even more potential bad news for you. The influential Commission on Immigration Reform recommended to Congress in June, 1995 that it entirely eliminate the 10,000 visas per year for the other worker category.

17

Fighting Job Discrimination

The Immigration Reform and Control Act of 1986 (I.R.C.A.) made it illegal for an employer to hire a foreign employee who is not a U.S. citizen or legal resident, or someone authorized to work by I.N.S. The employer sanctions law has made it very difficult for foreign citizens who are not authorized to work to survive in the U.S., and we have to be frank: it was a purpose of the law to discourage them from coming and to pressure them to go back home.

There is, in addition, an important component of the law which makes it possible for workers to sue employers who do not hire them, or who fire them, because they look or act "foreign." That part of the law was intended to promote fairness and protect the rights of legal workers, and has been a real benefit to many. This chapter will discuss what you can do if your employer violates your rights as a foreign citizen who is authorized to work in the U.S.

---

1. *Can the sanctions law protect me if I am not entitled to work legally in the U.S. ?*

No. This law does not help you if you are not authorized to work in the U.S.

However, even though the unauthorized worker is not protected by the sanctions law, you might be helped by other federal laws, such as the Fair Labor Standards Act. That law covers workers regardless of their immigration status.

2. *What are the actions of the employer that are considered to be unfair to me, if I am authorized to work?*

The law protects you if there is any discrimination against you in the process of hiring, or recruiting, or referring for a fee, or in the event of a firing.

3. *What if I get the job, but the boss does not promote me, because he doesn't like my foreign accent?*

I have to give you some bad news: the sanctions law covers hiring and firing, but does not cover failure to promote.

4. *If this law will not help me, is there another law that may?*

There may be. Title VII of the Civil Rights Act of 1964 makes it unlawful to discriminate on the basis of national origin, and that covers promotion as well as hiring and firing. However, it only applies to an employer of fifteen or more workers, so it will not help you if your employer operates a smaller business.

5. *If I am discriminated against, can I take my choice between the sanctions law and a different federal law?*

No. You must select one or the other. The sanctions law covers any employer of more than three workers, but does not include failure to promote. Title VII includes failure to promote, but does not cover an employer of fewer than fifteen workers.

6. *Does the job discrimination law protect a U.S. citizen as well as a foreign citizen who is a legal resident of the U.S.?*

Yes. It protects against discrimination on the basis of national origin and citizenship. An employer cannot refuse to hire workers because they are legal residents rather than U.S. citizens, or because they are U.S. citizens rather than legal residents.

7. *Is it legal for an employer to prefer U.S. citizens over legal residents in hiring?*
Yes, it is legal if the U.S. citizens and legal residents are equally qualified.

8. *What if the legal resident is better qualified?*
In that case, it is legal to hire a U.S. citizen instead of the legal resident for only one of three reasons:
- Hiring a U.S. citizen is necessary to comply with federal, state, or local law, or executive order;
- It is required by federal, state, or local government contract;
- The Attorney General determines that hiring a U.S. citizen is essential for an employer to do business with a federal, state, or local government agency.

9. *Does the job discrimination law apply to every employer?*
Yes, unless they employ three or fewer employees.

10. *If I believe I was not hired just because I look foreign, what can I do?*
You can file a complaint with the Office of Special Counsel.

11. *When do I have to file my complaint?*
Within 180 days (about six months) of the date of the occurrence (when your prospective employer told you that you were not going to be hired, or were going to be fired).

12. *Do I need a lawyer?*
A lawyer will certainly help, but you can file the complaint on your own.

13. *Where do I file my complaint?*
Mail it by certified mail, return receipt requested, to:
Office of Special Counsel for Immigration-related Employment Practices, P.O. Box 12728, Washington, D.C. 20038-7728.

14. *What do I put into the complaint?*
Give a play-by-play account of your application for the job, your interview, your rejection, and any conversation that you had with the interviewer or anyone else at the job site. Why do you believe that your national origin (your appearance, or accent) led to your rejection?
The Special Counsel will be looking for a believable account, not mere speculation or hunch on your part.

15. *How quickly will my complaint be decided?*
Within 120 days of receipt of the complaint.

16. *Can I file at the same time with the Equal Employment Opportunities Commission?*

No. Select one or the other. Keep the different ground rules in mind (see above, Questions 5, 9).

17. *Can you give me an example of someone who has won a case against an employer for job discrimination after bringing a complaint?*

Here's one example. In 1994 a case was settled between five Filipino security guards and their employer. The guards were either U.S. citizens or legal residents. After several years of work without any difficulties, all five were dismissed on the grounds that the employer had trouble understanding their accented English.

The employees filed a complaint with the U.S. Equal Employment Opportunities Commission (E.E.O.C.), under Title VII of the Civil Rights Act of 1964.

The employees were given their jobs back, and awarded a total of $87,500 ($17,500 per employee). In addition, the employer was required to remove all negative evaluations based on the firing incident and promised to prohibit any future discrimination based on accent.

18

Special Cases and Parole

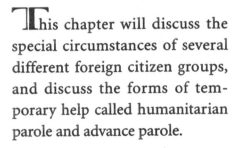

This chapter will discuss the special circumstances of several different foreign citizen groups, and discuss the forms of temporary help called humanitarian parole and advance parole.

---

1. *Does a Cuban citizen coming to the U.S. have a better chance of becoming a legal resident than the citizen of another country?*

Yes, but check Question 6 further on to see how this is changing. Here's the background.

The Cuban Refugee Adjustment Act, passed by Congress after Fidel Castro came to power in Cuba, established a favorable rule for Cubans (in effect, it encouraged Cubans to leave their homeland and choose a new home in the U.S., no doubt to the embarrassment of the Cuban government). The law provides that a Cuban citizen who is admitted to the U.S. or granted parole, and who resides in the U.S. for one year, may go ahead and apply for adjustment of status to legal residence in the U.S. There is no need, as there is for any other citizen group, to be petitioned for by a legal resident or U.S. citizen spouse, or by an employer, and have that petition approved, before being eligible to apply for adjustment.

Warning: a bill has been introduced in Congress by Senator Simpson that would repeal the act.

2. *What's the difference between being admitted and being paroled?*

To be admitted, you have to have a short term (nonimmigrant) visa, and be inspected and admitted by an immigration officer at the port of entry. You can also be admitted if the President takes action to admit you and other citizens of your country (see Question 6).

To be paroled, you do not have a nonimmigrant visa or a right to enter, but the U.S. government lets you in because that serves some humanitarian purpose.

3. *What is an example of humanitarian parole?*

In 1994, thousands of Cuban citizens fled their country in small boats and rafts, with the hope of reaching the U.S. and being allowed to remain here. If they were stopped on the high seas by the U.S. Coast Guard, they were moved either to the U.S. naval base at Guantanamo Bay (Cuba) or some other Caribbean location, and would not be paroled, and certainly not admitted, to the U.S.

One young woman, nine months pregnant, went into labor as her small boat approached the U.S. coast. The Coast Guard picked her up and flew her to a Miami hospital to give birth. The baby's birth in the U.S. made him a U.S. citizen. His mother, strictly speaking, had no right to be in the U.S., and, according to law, could have been sent to Guantanamo.

Fortunately, common sense and compassion won out, and she was paroled into the U.S. so that she could care for her U.S. citizen baby. One year later, she could apply for adjustment of status and become a legal resident.

4. *Didn't the U.S. and Cuba work out some kind of agreement after all of those thousands of Cubans headed for Miami in the summer of 1994?*

Yes, they did (but look ahead to Question 6 for the latest agreement).

Cuba agreed to take steps to discourage its citizens from fleeing to the U.S., and assured the U.S. that its discouragement of flight would not go so far as making attempted flight a crime, punishable by a prison sentence.

The U.S. agreed that it would allow a minimum of 20,000 Cubans per year to immigrate to the U.S.

5. *How will those 20,000 Cubans per year be selected?*

By a combination of methods. First of all, Cubans with a fear of persecution will be able to file asylum applications in Havana (look back to chapter 5, Question 1). Then there are the usual methods of having petitions filed by a close family member or by an employer, and approved by I.N.S.

In addition, the U.S. intends to use the parole power to let in deserving individuals. It started doing this by allowing into the U.S. persons in the detention camps who were age seventy or above, children not accompanied by adults, and persons with a serious medical condition.

6. *I hear that the President has announced some new policy on Cubans held in detention, or who will flee from Cuba in the future. What's that all about?*

On May 2, 1995 President Clinton announced a new policy concerning the treatment of Cuban citizens in detention now, or who may flee from Cuba in the future. The roughly 20,000 Cubans in detention at Guantanamo Bay will be admitted to the U.S., and will be able to adjust to legal residence a year later. But all Cubans who flee from Cuba in the future, and are picked up on the high seas by the U.S. Coast Guard, will be returned to Cuba, after a ship-board inquiry (lawyers are very unhappy about this way of deciding a case) to see whether they are political refugees. Once back in Cuba, they can assert at asylum claim at the U.S. interests section office in Havana.

The Cuban Adjustment Act is still in effect: only Congress has the authority to amend or repeal that law. Therefore, a Cuban citizen who actually reaches shore without interception, and who remains on U.S. soil for a year, will still be able to adjust to legal residence one year after arrival. But the new Presidential policy is designed to block a large-scale exodus from Cuba to the U.S., and, as we go to press, the interceptions on the high seas and the forcible returns are being implemented.

7. *I am a Haitian citizen, and I have been granted parole. Can I adjust to legal residence after one year of residing in the U.S.?*

No. That special one-year-later adjustment applies only to Cubans. It does not apply to Haitians, or to citizens of any other country of the world.

8. *That's too bad. But if I continue living in the U.S. for seven years in my parole status, can I then apply for suspension of deportation, and in that way obtain legal residence?*

No. Suspension of deportation applies to a foreign citizen who has been physically present in the U.S. for at least seven years.

9. *Won't I fit that definition in seven years? I plan to settle in Miami, and I do not intend to leave the U.S. during the next seven years.*

No, you will not fit that definition.

Now I have to tell you something that you may not believe, even after checking it out with a good immigration lawyer.

When you are paroled into the U.S., you do not formally enter the U.S. and start to establish physical presence here. Instead, from a legal point of view, you are still sitting on the rickety boat or raft that brought you toward Miami, before you were stopped by the U.S. Coast Guard. Or you are still sitting on the plane that brought you to the port of entry.

Before you can start clocking days, months, and years of physical presence in the U.S., you have to either be admitted by an immigration officer at the port of entry, or you have to have entered the U.S. without inspection by crossing the border with Canada or Mexico. You did not formally enter the U.S., either legally or illegally. Therefore, you can be here for seven or seventeen years, and you will still be regarded as sitting off shore.

10. *If that's the case, what's good about being on humanitarian parole?*

There are lots of good things about it. For one thing, you can apply for permission to work legally in the U.S. You write (c)(11) (paroled in the public interest) at box 16 of the new Form I-765 Application for Employment Authorization. New I.N.S. rules require that the I-765 application, with photos and fingerprints, be submitted at your local I.N.S. office. The Employment Authorization Document (E.A.D.), either mailed out or picked up by you at the local office, will be valid for one year.

And, if you are unmarried, you can hope that you will meet and marry in good faith a U.S. citizen or legal resident, who can file a petition for you that may lead to your legal residence (see chapter 8 for more on this procedure).

11. *I have a green card. My daughter in the home country is married. It will take me years to get to become a U.S. citizen and be able to petition for her. I am getting old, and am afraid I will never be able to get her to the U.S. Can she get humanitarian parole to come here to be with me?*

In all likelihood, the answer is "No." Humanitarian parole is described as an extraordinary measure, and it cannot be used to short-cut the normal delays of petitioning for a close relative. If it were a short-cut, many brothers and sisters of U.S. citizens would be coming here on parole, rather than sitting in the home countries and waiting for ten to twenty years for an immigrant visa to be available to them. But that is not happening.

You are right that you cannot file a petition now: a green card holder cannot petition for a married son or daughter. I.N.S. will be rather hard boiled about this. If you must see your daughter, they will ask, why not take a trip to the home country and visit her there?

Your case, at the moment, is not a good one for humanitarian parole.

This could change. Humanitarian parole will not be granted if a case can be satisfactorily resolved through normal channels. But if for some reason it becomes impossible for you to travel to the home country, then you will explain to I.N.S. that the normal waiting procedures will not satisfactorily resolve the case, and that it is an emergency that only a grant of parole will cure.

In such a case, parole may be granted.

12. *If I see that emergency coming, what do I do to apply for humanitarian parole for my daughter?*

You use the same form that we discussed in chapter 2, Question 23, when someone with a green card has to remain outside the U.S. for more than a year. It is the Form I-131 Application for Travel Document, with payment to I.N.S. of $70. What is referred to as humanitarian parole is a special form of something called advance parole. Your daughter, who is outside the U.S., may submit the application for herself, or you may submit it on her behalf.

You must include a Form I-134 Affidavit of Support to explain how you will support your daughter, if she is granted humanitarian parole.

Since your daughter is outside the U.S., the Form I-131 does not go to the local I.N.S. office, but to: USINS, Office of International Affairs and Parole, 425 I Street NW, Room 1203, Washington, DC 20536.

While this is going on, make sure to take every step to file for naturalization as soon as you are eligible. I.N.S. wants to see that you are not just sitting back and asking for a big favor.

13. *I was one of the Chinese citizens who traveled to the U.S. aboard the Golden Venture in 1992. Over two years later, I am still in I.N.S. detention. How long will this go on?*

I gather that you were picked up on the beach and placed in I.N.S. detention. You are being held for what are called exclusion proceedings. Even though you set foot on a sandy beach in New York, you did not enter the U.S., from a legal point of view. According to law, you can be held in I.N.S. detention until exclusion proceedings against you are completed. If your case is still pending, that is probably because you have applied for asylum, and have run into delays related to the difficulties of obtaining a lawyer of your choice while in detention.

You would like to be released while your case is pending, but the reasons for release from detention (called parole) are very strict.

14. *How do I qualify to be released on parole?*

According to I.N.S. rules, you may be paroled only if:
- You have a serious medical condition;
- You are a woman and are pregnant;
- You are a juvenile (under age fourteen);
- You have close family members in the U.S. who are either U.S. citizens or legal residents, and they have filed a visa petition for you;
- You will be a witness in legal proceedings (for example, if you will be a witness against the smugglers who planned and executed the voyage of the Golden Venture);
- Your continued detention is not in the public interest (there would have to be some very unusual favorable factor to cause I.N.S. to parole you for this reason).

If you are a single young man in good health, your chances of being paroled by I.N.S. are close to zero. But a judge might just possibly see things differently.

15. *Since jumping for my life from the Golden Venture, I have been bounced like a ping-pong ball all around the U.S., from New York to Pennsylvania to Louisiana. The lawyer I found in New York has not been able to follow me around, and I have not found another whom I like. Is it legal for the I.N.S. to do this to me?*

Yes, it is. There is an old law case, which has never been overturned, that says that whatever Congress decides to do with a foreign citizen who is knocking at the gates, as you are, is due process so far as you are concerned. Bouncing you around like a ping-pong ball, which makes it very hard for you to get a lawyer of your choice, is terrible, but not illegal.

As we go to press, two contradictory things are occurring. On the one hand, significant numbers of passengers from the Golden Venture, discouraged by their long detention, the inability to be paroled, and the small chance of winning their cases, have abandoned their asylum claims and accepted deportation to China.

On the other hand, a hope for parole has been raised by a decision by a U.S. District Court judge on May 17, 1995 that a Golden Venture detainee who had set foot on the Long Island beach in 1992 had actually entered the U.S., and should be held not in exclusion proceedings, but in deportation proceedings. As such, she would be eligible to be released, if she could raise the money to be bonded out. The I.N.S., which has insisted all along that setting foot on the sand did not constitute entry, will undoubtedly appeal the decision. The fate of the Golden Venture passengers remains uncertain.

16. *I am not under deportation proceedings, or in I.N.S. detention. I have applied for asylum, and, although several years have gone by, I have not yet been called by I.N.S. for an interview. I am now a senior in college in the U.S., and about to graduate with honors. I have entered a nationwide competition, and won an award from the National Institute for Health. It entails a summer of research abroad. Is there some way that I can get permission to leave the U.S. and then return?*

Yes. You file for what is called advance parole, and the district office should give it to you if you have a very good personal or professional reason for needing it.

You use Form 1-131 Application for Travel Document (look back to chapter 2, Questions 19-22 for a different use of this form), with payment to I.N.S. of $70. Instructions to the form state that if you in the U.S. you may apply for an advance parole document if you seek to travel abroad for emergent personal or bona fide business reasons. Instructions further state that you will not get it if you have been placed under deportation proceedings. This does not apply to you. You have made what is called an affirmative asylum application, and will eventually be interviewed by I.N.S. A deportation proceeding would not be in your future unless I.N.S. first denies your application.

17. *If I am granted advance parole to leave the U.S. and then return a few months later, can I make a short stop in my home country to visit my family?*

No. If your home country is where you fear persecution, according to your asylum application, a return home will have the effect of an abandonment of your asylum application (and you will at the same time lose your permission to return to the U.S.).

18. *Very good. I am able to file the form. But do I have any chance of having my application accepted?*

You certainly do have a good chance. You must emphasize, in a cover letter, that you have been an outstanding student (get letters from the college so stating), that the work is very important to your career, that the departure is short, and that the college wants you to go. With a very strong letter from your college, requesting that you be granted permission to depart briefly and then return, you have a very good chance.

You will be scheduled to come to the district office with a valid passport, and the advance parole paper will be handed to you "at the counter" of the refugee section. A formal interview with an immigration examiner is probably not required.

19. *My passport from the country that persecuted me has expired. Is that going to be a problem for me?*

Yes. If you do not have a valid passport, I.N.S. will not give you advance parole. Your asylum lawyer may be reluctant to have you renew your passport, since any contact with your home government has a tendency to weaken the believability of your asylum claim. But if the summer research will significantly enhance your career options, renewing the passport and taking advantage of the advance parole is something you may not want to sacrifice.

Your lawyer will advise you of a potential disadvantage of obtaining advance parole while your asylum application is pending: if I.N.S. denies your application, it may then place you not under deportation proceedings, but under exclusion proceedings, which would make life a lot more difficult for you. If this happens, your lawyer's creativity will have to come to the fore.

20. *I have a green card. My fourteen year old son, a Haitian citizen, fled his home-land a year ago, was picked up by the U.S. Coast Guard and placed at Guantanamo Bay, Cuba. Is he going to be kept there indefinitely, or sent back to Haiti?*

Neither of those two alternatives, according to a recent statement by the State Department. Since your son has a parent in the U.S. in legal resident status who can care for him, it is very likely that he will be paroled into the U.S. to your care. You will then be able (if you haven't already) to file a Preference 2A petition for him. It will take about three years before an immigrant visa will be available to him, so that he can adjust status in the U.S. During that time you will request that his parole status be continued until he can have his adjustment interview and get a green card.

Haitian children without parents in the U.S. in legal resident status are being sent back to Haiti.

19

If You Need Public Benefits

This chapter will discuss the public benefits that are available to foreign citizens, called aliens by the immigration law. Since the new Congress is proposing to reduce the benefits that foreign citizens now enjoy, our discussion will alternate between the way things now are, and the way they are likely to be in the near future.

---

1. *Are there any public benefits that undocumented foreign citizens are entitled to?*

As we go to press, foreign citizens without documents (sometimes referred to as illegal aliens) are generally entitled to immunizations, emergency medical treatment, and the W.I.C. program (Women, Infants, and Children), providing nutritional care connected with childbirth.

2. *Are there plans to do away with these benefits?*

There certainly are. A bill passed by the House of Representatives March 24, 1995, numbered H.R. 1214, would do away with any federal benefits for the so-called "illegal alien."

Furthermore, the proposed bill would prohibit states and localities from spending their own money on nonemergency benefits to the undocumented, a striking example of the federal government dictating to the states when it comes to immigrants.

3. *What are the public benefit programs that legal residents (green card holders) are now eligible to apply for, if they can prove economic need?*

The important benefit programs that the legal resident may be eligible for include:

Non-emergency Medicaid; Pre-natal care; Community health center services; W.I.C. (nutritional supplements for women and infants); A.F.D.C. (Aid to Families with Dependent Children); School lunches; Foster care and adoption assistance; Screening for lead poisoning in infants and children; S.S.I. (Supplemental Security Income to assist the elderly and disabled); Public housing; Legal aid; Emergency food and shelter.

4. *Is the new Congress proposing to eliminate any of these programs for foreign citizens who are legal residents?*

The bill passed by the House of Representatives in March, called the Personal Responsibility Act, would eliminate all of them.

5. *Is there an exception that allows some legal residents to receive some benefits?*

Yes. Legal residents who are excepted from the blanket prohibition on receiving benefits are: those over age 75 who have been in legal resident status for over five years; refugees who have been in that status for less than five years (this does not apply to persons granted asylum in the U.S., who would be excluded from benefits); legal residents who are veterans of military service, and their spouses and unmarried dependents; legal residents with mental disorders or physical impairments so severe that they could not pass the naturalization exam.

6. *I read somewhere that the S.S.I. (Supplemental Security Income) program is a rip-off. Elderly immigrants who are able to work are quitting their jobs and using the program as a form of retirement, paid for by me and other U.S. taxpayers. What's the story on S.S.I.?*

Let's look at the whole picture, as described for us by a report in January, 1995 from the General Accounting Office (G.A.O.), an independent body that investigates and reports to Congress.

S.S.I. was established by Congress in 1972 to provide minimum subsistence to the elderly, blind, and disabled who were not able to draw Social Security benefits. One had to be a U.S. citizen or legal resident (green card holder) to be eligible to apply. Since 1986 the benefits paid to the elderly, blind, and disabled has more than doubled. According to the G.A.O. report: "Benefits for the disabled accounted for almost 100% of this increase." Legal resident foreign citizens who choose not to work, apparently, are not a significant factor in the doubling of benefits paid since 1986.

It is important to note, from the report, that legal immigrants do not take, by any means, the lion's share of S.S.I. benefits. In 1982, they took three percent of the total S.S.I. benefit outlay. In 1986, the Immigration Reform and Control Act (I.R.C.A.) resulted in the legalization of three million foreign citizens: three million new green card holders, some of them elderly, some of them disabled. Probably largely as a result of the new legal immigrants, the immigrant share of S.S.I. benefits rose to 11% by 1993, still a rather small share of the total.

There is an additional reason to question the alleged rip-off of the program by legal residents. The income of the close relative who petitioned for the foreign citizen is "deemed" to be part of their income for three years, which will put many above the eligibility level. During the period January 1994 to September 1996 the "deeming" period is extended from three to five years.

Some members of Congress are looking for a more drastic solution. Since it is the elderly parent of the U.S. citizen petitioner who is using S.S.I., let's just remove parents from the immediate relative category. U.S. children: forget about bringing your parents to the U.S.!

That legislation, if it gets anywhere, would wreck havoc with traditional notions of family reunification, and put foreign citizen parents beyond the pale of "family values." Is that what we really want to do?

7. *I became a legal resident as a result of a petition by my spouse. His income is considered ("deemed") to be part of mine, so that I cannot qualify for benefits unless our joint income falls below a certain level. And this deeming goes on for three years. Does that stay the same under this new proposal?*

No. Under the new bill, the deeming continues indefinitely, or until you become naturalized, and goes so far as to include state and local programs that do not even use federal funds.

8. *Is the I.N.S. behind this new piece of legislation?*

No. The I.N.S. Commissioner opposes reducing or eliminating benefits to legal residents, and the making of "discriminatory" distinctions between legal residents and U.S. citizens when it comes to eligibility for public benefits. This opposition from the agency responsible for immigration suggests that the final bill may be quite different from the one passed by the House. Congress may, at the end of the road, decide to leave legal residents alone, and concentrate instead on the foreign citizen who has entered the U.S. without inspection, and the foreign citizen who has committed crimes in the U.S.

9. *I am a resident of the state of California. I do not have legal papers, and neither* *do my two children, who live with me and attend public school. What does Proposition 187 mean for us?*

Keep this in mind: the federal courts have enjoined (prevented) agencies of the state from applying Proposition 187 for the foreseeable future.

But if the law were to go into effect in the future, it would be very bad news for you and your children. The school that your children attend would be required to verify the immigration status of your children. Discovering that they were not in legal status, the school would have to report this fact to the I.N.S., and that agency could then start deportation proceedings against them. To make matters even worse, the school would have to verify your status (it is very hard to see what purpose this serves, other than to discourage the parent from ever visiting her child's school), and report its findings to I.N.S.

If you and your children visit a public health clinic to receive medical care, the clinic has to perform the same function as the school: verify the immigration status of child and parent, and report the findings of a lack of legal status to the I.N.S.

Even though Proposition 187 is now held up as a result of lawsuits, it is extremely disturbing to think about its probable consequences, if the courts finally decide that it is legal and may be implemented. What happens if a foreign citizen who lacks legal status develops a dangerous contagious disease like infectious tuberculosis, and dares not visit a clinic to get a proper diagnosis and treatment? What happens to the sick person without legal status, and what happens to those he comes in close contact with, who may include children, of whatever immigration status? The virus does not stop to verify immigration status, and it seems irrational, from a public health perspective, to prohibit medical treatment to those in the United States who need it, irrespective of their immigration status.

We also have to wonder whether the U.S. Congress may pass a federal law that will imitate some features of Proposition 187, and that will apply to the entire nation.

10. *Has the passage of Proposition 187 already scared people away from health clinics?*

Yes. A report published in early 1995 by a medical journal found that California state hospitals and health clinics have reported a 20% decline in requests for medical services. Usage of vitally important pre-natal clinics has dropped by 30%.

Supporters of Proposition 187 applaud these statistics. Advocates for immigrants shudder at their implications from a public health point of view, and from the point of view of our society's traditional ethical concern for the most vulnerable among us.

11. *Has any politician pointed out that such a law, in addition to being hard hearted, is just impractical, and cannot realistically be implemented?*

Yes. That point was made by Rudolph Giuliani, Major of the City of New York, in an article published in the weekly newspaper *The Irish Voice.*

The Mayor starts off by discussing New York City's long-standing policy of reporting foreign citizens engaged in criminal activity to I.N.S., but not taking note of the immigration status of persons seeking benefits in terms of education, health care, or help from the police or fire departments. He points out that a law like Proposition 187 would require the city to report to I.N.S. "the names of illegal aliens who send their children to public schools, seek medical care or report crime. The threat of deportation understandably would induce many families to forego needed medical care, keep their children out of school, and refuse to report crimes or act as witnesses in criminal cases."

A central point made by the Mayor is that the huge numbers of children and parents reported to I.N.S. would overwhelm the agency, distract it from the important task of deporting criminal aliens, and would have no effect on illegal immigration. Mr. Giuliani cites these estimated figures: 100,000-200,000 names of foreign citizen parents whose children are in the public schools; 40,000-50,000 names of foreign citizens seeking medical treatment; 200,000-300,000 names of foreign citizens who report crimes. The Mayor's conclusion: "Dumping an additional 340,000-550,000 names on the I.N.S. would bury the Service in paperwork. Lacking sufficient numbers of agents, the I.N.S. is able to process less than five percent of the names New York City now submits."

The Mayor's next two paragraphs are worth quoting in full.

> While doing nothing to impede illegal immigration, the law would drive law-abiding men, women , and children underground into lives of fear and uncertainty. And the safety and well-being of every New Yorker would be threatened.
>
> Thousands of children, kept out of school by fearful parents, would wind up on our city's streets. Communicable diseases would spread unchecked, as illegal immigrants eschewed medical attention. Criminals would enjoy a windfall, as illegal immigrants, avoiding contact with the police, refused to report crime.

It seems to this observer that the immigrant scapegoating that a law like Proposition 187 embodies will not have the effect of prompting undocumented foreign citizens to pull up stakes and return to their troubled home countries. But it will sow the seeds of misery among that population, and that misery, soon enough, will come back to haunt those of us who happen, by an accident or birth or lucky circumstance, to be in lawful immigration status.

12. *Has any other state done anything like, or unlike, what California did?*

Yes. The state legislature of New Mexico passed a resolution (called "Memorial") on March 17, 1995 in which they acknowledge their state's debt to its immigrants, and roundly reject the "divisiveness" that they see as a product of California's Proposition 187. Copies of the "Memorial" were sent to the I.N.S., President Clinton, the New Mexico Congressional delegation, and the Chairmen of the Judiciary Committees of the U.S. Senate and House of Representatives.

Ways to Become a Citizen

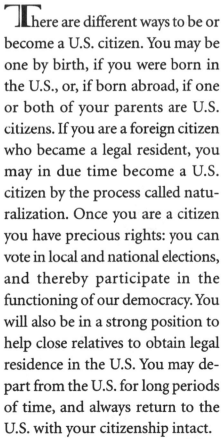

There are different ways to be or become a U.S. citizen. You may be one by birth, if you were born in the U.S., or, if born abroad, if one or both of your parents are U.S. citizens. If you are a foreign citizen who became a legal resident, you may in due time become a U.S. citizen by the process called naturalization. Once you are a citizen you have precious rights: you can vote in local and national elections, and thereby participate in the functioning of our democracy. You will also be in a strong position to help close relatives to obtain legal residence in the U.S. You may depart from the U.S. for long periods of time, and always return to the U.S. with your citizenship intact.

As a citizen, you are immune from the immigrant scapegoating that seems to be a byproduct of hard economic times in the U.S. You will not be in danger of losing whatever public benefits you are entitled to, as you might be if you remained a non-citizen. Our suggestion: apply for naturalization when eligible to do so!

This chapter will review the various ways to be or become a citizen.

---

1. *I crossed the border between the U.S. and an adjoining country when I was nine months pregnant. I gave birth to my baby a week later. How can I be sure that she is a U.S. citizen by birth?*

Because it says so in the U.S. Constitution.

Section 1 of the Fourteenth Amendment states: "All persons born or naturalized in the United States, and subject to the jurisdiction thereof, are citizens of the United States."

This important amendment was passed after the American Civil War, to make it clear that former African-American slaves were now free U.S. citizens, by reason of their birth in the U.S.

2. *The governor of my state wants to change that, so that children of foreign citizens who are born here are not U.S. citizens, but are just "aliens" who can be sent back to the country where I was born. Can he do that?*

No. Not unless the Fourteenth Amendment is repealed or amended.

For an amendment of the U.S. Constitution to take effect, it must be proposed by ⅔ of the U.S. House of Representatives and ⅔ of the U.S. Senate, and then ratified by ¾ of the state legislatures. Although proposing amendments to the U.S. Constitution is something that the current Congress is not shy about doing, there is, as we go to press, no indication that it is ready to repeal or amend the Fourteenth Amendment. It therefore stands as an obstacle to whatever action your governor or state legislature might take to remove citizenship status from children of foreign citizens who are born in the U.S.

3. *My husband and I are both U.S. citizens. We were living abroad for two years while I was studying at a foreign university for a degree. I gave birth to our child during that period of time abroad. Can I be sure that he is a U.S. citizen by birth?*

Yes, provided that one of you maintained a U.S. residence before the child's birth.

A residence is defined as your principal place of abode, and it can be shown by proof of home ownership or a copy of an apartment lease. U.S. residence can also be shown by copies of U.S. tax returns during the two year period of your study abroad.

4. *Can I get confirmation of my son's U.S. citizenship from the U.S. government?*

Yes. You should visit the U.S. Consulate in the foreign country where you are now staying. Show the following:

- Proof of your U.S. citizenship;
- Proof of your husband's U.S. citizenship;
- Your child's birth certificate and any necessary translation;
- Proof that you or your husband were U.S. residents before your child's birth.

The consular officer will give you a document confirming the U.S. citizenship of your child, and you can use that to get him a U.S. passport for travel back to the U.S.

5. *I am a U.S. citizen, and my wife is a legal resident (has a green card). We have been living together in the U.S. for about three years. My wife went to her home country last month to visit her family, and while there gave birth to our child. Is our child a U.S. citizen?*

That depends. The law is interested in knowing how close and long term your connection has been to the U.S. For your child to be qualified as a citizen from birth, you need to prove that you have been physically present in the U.S. for the past five years.

6. *What does it mean to be physically present in the United States?*

It is a lot more demanding, and harder to prove, than just showing residence in the U.S.

It means that you have to have been here every day of that five year period, except for very short absences that are described as brief, casual, and innocent, and that do not meaningfully interrupt your physical presence in the States.

For example, if you took a short vacation to visit your wife's family in her home country, that would not interrupt your physical presence here. But if you took on some business venture that kept you out of the U.S. for six months or so, that would break your physical presence here.

A word of caution may be in order: try to plan your business or vacation schedules so that your children are born in the U.S., not abroad. It really makes life much easier when you have the Fourteenth Amendment on your side, assuring you that children born in the U.S. are U.S. citizens.

7. *After the birth of our child abroad, what do we do to establish that she is a U.S. citizen by birth?*

Your wife should visit the U.S. Consulate in her home country, and show:

- Her green card as proof of legal resident status;
- A copy of your birth or naturalization certificate to prove your U.S. citizen status;
- A copy of your child's birth certificate and any necessary translation;
- Proof that you have been physically present in the U.S. for the past five years.

Start with the past five years of income tax returns, records of your bank accounts, and of your payment of utility bills, showing your addresses for the last five years. She should present a photocopy of your U.S. passport, showing that there were only a few very short term departures from the U.S. during the past five years.

The consular officer should then be able to provide your wife with a document showing that your daughter is a U.S. citizen, and enabling her to get a U.S. passport for your child.

8. *If I cannot prove that I was physically present in the U.S. for five years before our child's birth, is there any other way to make her a U.S. citizen by birth?*

Yes. You should first file an immediate relative petition for your child and help her become a legal resident. Your wife should then, as soon as she is eligible, file her application to become a naturalized citizen (she must be naturalized before your child turns eighteen). Here's what the law says:

If your wife becomes a naturalized citizen before your child turns eighteen years of age, and if your child, as a legal resident, has been residing in the U.S. with her at the time that she (your wife) is naturalized, the child retroactively becomes a U.S. citizen by birth.

Put it this way: your child has "two bites of the apple" of citizenship, the first at the time of her birth abroad to a legal resident mother and U.S. citizen father, and the second later when her legal resident mother becomes a naturalized citizen.

9. *I read somewhere that there is a new law that will give some people "instant citizenship." What is that all about?*

That is something very specific and rather narrow. It can help some hundreds or thousands of people who are now in their sixties or older, but it will not mean that a flood of foreign citizens will be able to wave a magic wand and instantly become U.S. citizens.

10. *Who will it help?*

If you were born abroad (outside the U.S.) before May 24, 1934 of a U.S. citizen mother and non-citizen father, you will now be regarded as a U.S. citizen from birth, provided that your mother resided in the U.S. before your birth.

11. *Assuming that I can show birth abroad before May 24, 1934 to a U.S. citizen mother, and that my mother resided in the U.S. before my birth, are there any bars to my citizenship?*

You are barred if you participated in Nazi persecutions (1933-45) or engaged in genocide.

12. *What if I was born abroad before May 24, 1934 to a U.S. citizen father and foreign citizen mother? Am I out of luck?*

On the contrary. You are a U.S. citizen from birth, and that law has been in effect for some time. What the new law does is give the U.S. citizen mother as much "clout" (ability to confer citizenship) as the father. That makes a lot of sense, and is long overdue. After all, who is it who gives birth to the child?

13. *I got my green card as a result of a petition filed by my spouse, a legal resident. How soon after getting the card can I file for naturalization?*

You file for naturalization five years after the date printed on your green card as the date of issue.

14. *Does the five year waiting period apply to everyone who becomes a legal resident?*

Five years from the date of issue on the green card is the rule for everyone except:

Someone who got the card as the result of a petition by a U.S. citizen spouse, where the waiting time is three years, and someone helped by a special law like the Cuban-Haitian Adjustment Act of 1986, where those who were adjusted to legal resident status could file for naturalization immediately.

15. *Is there a problem if I apply for naturalization ahead of time?*

Whether you have a three or five year wait to your eligibility date, I.N.S. will let you apply up to three months before that date. If you apply earlier than that, the Service will return your application with your payment, and advise you to wait.

To reassure I.N.S. that you are not applying ahead of time, you should enclose a photocopy of both sides of your green card with your application The date of issue on the face of the card will prove that you are not applying more than three months ahead of schedule.

As we go to press, the waiting time in most districts between filing the application and having the interview is between nine and twelve months.

16. *During that three (or five) year waiting period, I made several long trips to the home country to visit my family. How much of that three (or five) years did I actually have to be in the U.S.?*

Be careful. You have to show that you were physically present in the U.S. for one day more than ½ of that three (or five) year period (in other words, for one day more than 1½ years, or one day more than 2½ years, depending on whether your waiting period is three or five years).

Remember the very demanding standard for proving physical presence: you have to show that you were in the U. S. every day of the required period, except for very brief departures (so-called brief, casual, and innocent departures).

17. *During my three (or five) year waiting period, I had a family emergency in the* *home country and had to go back there for more than a year. Can I still file for naturalization three (or five) years after my green card was issued?*

No. A departure from the U.S. for more than a year will break the three (or five) year waiting period.

18. *If the waiting period is broken, do I have to start from the beginning and wait for an entire unbroken three (or five) year period of continuous residence?*

No. What you need to do is to wait for two years (or four years) and a day, and then file your application for naturalization. I.N.S. will pretend that your allowable period of departure of up to one year was taken at the start of the new three (or five) year period, so that a continuous period of two (or four) years and a day will fully satisfy the residence requirement.

19. *How long do I have to reside in my state before filing an application for naturalization?*

Three months.

20. *After I file my application, do I have to be physically present in the U.S. (in the U.S. every day of the week and every week of the month) until I am sworn in as a citizen?*

No. You merely have to reside continuously in the U.S. from the time of filing until the time of swearing in. During that period of time, you can make departures from the U.S., and they do not have to be extremely brief.

21. *What is the I.N.S. form that I use to apply for naturalization, and what is the fee?*

You use the Form N-400 Application for Naturalization, with payment of $95 to "Immigration and Naturalization Service."

You must also submit:
- Photocopy of both sides of Form I-551 Alien Registration card (green card);
- Form FD-258 Fingerprint chart (two samples, to make sure that at least one of them can be read by the F.B.I. to confirm that you do not have a criminal record);
- Four identical color photos (head and shoulders, ¾ view looking to left, right ear visible, name and A-number printed on the back with Number 2 pencil).

22. *What is the rule on knowing English and U.S. history?*

The general rule is that you must be able to read, write, and speak ordinary English, and know some basic facts about U.S. history and government. The examiner will give you a short paragraph to read out loud, and will dictate a sentence for you to write and properly spell. You will be asked ten questions about U.S. history and government, and must answer seven correctly to pass the test. If you fail any part of the test, you will be given a chance to return within ninety days and take the test again, without having to pay a new fee. To prepare for the U.S. history and government test, you should obtain, from any immigration lawyer or organization that assists foreign citizens, the 100 Questions and Answers that I.N.S. made available to applicants for legalization ("amnesty") in 1986. They will serve you well on your naturalization test.

You are excused from the English test (but not the history test) if you are fifty years old or older, and have been a legal resident for at least twenty years, or are fifty-five or above and have been a legal resident for at least fifteen years. In either of these cases, the history test will be given in your language.

According to a new rule, you will be in effect excused from both the English and history test if you are at least sixty-five, and have been a legal resident for at least twenty years. I.N.S. has published and will widely distribute the ten rather easy questions that will be asked on U.S. history, in the language of your choice, and you must get six of them right.

23. *Someone told me that I have to show something called* good moral character *if I want to be a citizen. What is that?*

We will give some specific examples, in response to questions that follow. If you think that you have a problem with so-called good moral character, get yourself a good immigration lawyer to evaluate your situation.

24. *When, as a legal resident, I filed a petition for my child, I cheated. I said that she was unmarried, when in fact she was married. Is that a problem for me?*

Yes. You lied to the I.N.S. in order to get an immigration benefit for your child. You knew that you could not file a petition for a married child: only a U.S. citizen can do that. And so you pretended that she was unmarried.

If the I.N.S. finds out about this, it will reject your application for naturalization on the ground that you lack good moral character. The Service can also rescind (take back) your petition for your child, if it was mistakenly granted in the first place on the basis of false information that you provided to them.

25. *When I had been a legal resident for ten years, I was convicted of drug trafficking. I.N.S. tried to deport me. But the immigration judge granted my application for relief from deportation because of my U.S. citizen spouse and children, and the fact that I was rehabilitated (I had cut my ties to the drug world, and was doing volunteer work to help drug addicts). Can I go ahead and apply now to become a U.S. citizen?*

No. You are very lucky that the immigration judge gave you the benefit of the doubt and allowed you to remain here as a legal resident. But it will be difficult for you to take the next step and become a citizen.

You cannot show good moral character and be eligible for naturalization if you committed what is called an aggravated felony during the period of your legal residence. And drug trafficking (the sale of a controlled substance) has been labeled as an aggravated felony. You can kiss that five year period of legal residence good-bye.

If you stay on the "right road" for the next period of years, you should try again, and hope that the Service will give more weight to the recent years than to the distant past.

26. *When I was a legal resident, I was convicted of a gambling offense. I.N.S. never placed me under deportation proceedings for that, and I was told by a lawyer that the gambling conviction would not lead to my deportation. Since it is a pretty minor thing, it will not prevent me from being naturalized, will it?*

That depends. If it is a one-time offense, and a minor one, you can still be naturalized and become a U.S. citizen. But if it looks as if you made your living, during the three or five years of legal residence, from illegal gambling activities, that will show a lack of good moral character, and ruin your chances of becoming a U.S. citizen. The fact that illegal gambling does not make you deportable is not relevant: you can avoid deportation, but still be blocked from naturalization.

27. *I have not paid income taxes every year that I have been a legal resident. Will that prevent me from becoming a U.S. citizen?*

It may. Although the I.N.S. is not the I.R.S. (Internal Revenue Service), it is likely to regard a failure to pay taxes as a failure to show good moral character. Although failure to pay taxes is not listed as one of those specific actions that rule out good moral character, the immigration law points out that the list is just an illustration, it does not pretend to list each and every action that rules out good moral character.

There is a question on the Form N-400 Application for Naturalization (Part 7, Question 8) that asks whether you have failed to file a Federal Tax return since becoming a legal resident. If your answer is "Yes," I suggest that you make every effort to file now for the year or years that you missed, and pay whatever back taxes (and penalty and interest) that you may owe.

If you do not, you will be inviting a rejection of your naturalization application.

28. *Are some examiners more interested in my tax record than others?*

Examiners generally ask about your tax record, but they vary in their degree of interest.

One examiner may be rather casual and ask, "Do you pay your taxes?", and be satisfied with a "Yes" answer. More typically, an examiner may want to see copies of the two or three most recent years of your federal and state tax returns.

It is best to play it conservative. Assume that you will be asked to show copies of your recent returns, and make sure that you have them to show.

29. *Will the I.N.S. give me special treatment if I have done something for the U.S. recently?*

It's not up to I.N.S. to do that. It is something that the President can do, and has done with respect to foreign citizens who have served in particular wars. Their naturalization applications may be expedited, which means that their waiting period in legal resident status can be cut short.

This was done by Presidential Executive Order on November 22, 1994 with respect to those who were in the armed forces during the period of the Gulf War (August 2, 1990 to April 11, 1991). It is not necessary to have actually served in the Gulf War, just to have been in the armed forces during the relevant time period.

30. *I have been a legal resident for six years. I joined the army three years ago (there was no war going on at that time). I couldn't get used to army life, and I went A.W.O.L. (Absent Without Leave) for several months during my tour of duty. I was not court martialed, but I was given a less than honorable discharge. Will I still have a chance of becoming a citizen?*

This is going to be a very close call.

During wartime, an absence without leave from the armed forces will cancel your eligibility to become a citizen, if the A.W.O.L. results in a court martial. Your absence was during peacetime, and did not result in a court martial.

This means that there is still a razor-thin chance that you could be naturalized. You will still need to prove a record of good moral character, and going A.W.O.L. while a legal resident, while not specifically listed as a cancellation of good moral character, does not exactly back it up.

Let's hope that you have lots of positives to outweigh this strong negative in your background.

31. *Which foreign citizens are required to register with the Selective Service Administration?*

The law requires that every young man who is a U.S. citizen, "and every other male person residing in the United States," register with Selective Service between the ages of eighteen and twenty-six.

This is sometimes called "registering for the draft," although there has not been a draft (required military service) since the Vietnam War period of the mid-1960s and early 1970s. If there ever is a draft in the future, current legal concepts of Equal Protection under the laws may require that young women, as well as young men, be required to register for the draft and serve in the armed forces. From a political point of view, this makes it unlikely that Congress will be in a hurry to reintroduce the draft.

32. *Are there any foreign citizens who are not required to register with Selective Service?*

You are not required to register if you are in nonimmigrant status, so long as you remain in valid status.

33. *What if I become an overstay, or violate my status by working without permission. Am I then required to register?*

Yes.

34. *What if I entered without inspection by crossing the border, and the I.N.S. placed me under deportation proceedings? Am I required to register?*

If you are bonded out of I.N.S. detention, and are between the ages of eighteen and twenty-six, you must register.

35. *What procedure do I follow to register with Selective Service?*

Go to any U.S. Post Office and pick up a registration form. Fill it out, and mail it to the Selective Service Administration by ordinary first class mail. You will be contacted and given a Selective Service number.

36. *I have been a legal resident for five years, and am getting ready to apply for naturalization. I didn't know that I was supposed to register for the draft, and I did not register. Is that going to cause me a problem?*

The government has apparently not learned about your failure to register, but it will learn about it from your response to Question 5 on Form N-400: "Have you ever failed to comply with the Selective Service Laws?" There is a potential criminal prosecution for failure to register, and, unless it is excused, that failure will also make you ineligible for naturalization.

37. *How can my failure to register be excused?*

You know the general rule that ignorance of the law does not excuse failure to comply. However, there may be some facts that might persuade I.N.S. to excuse you. You have to convince I.N.S. that your failure to register was not willful (you did not know about the law and then deliberately decide to ignore it). You might state (if this is true) that you have complied with every advice that you have ever received from any I.N.S. officer, but that, at the time of becoming a legal resident, you were never informed by the immigration examiner that you had any obligation to register with Selective Service, and never received any written advice to that effect from the government.

You might also state (if it is true) that, had you known about the law, of course you would have complied with it. You very much regret your inadvertent failure to register, and you hope and pray that you can now become a citizen and assume all the serious obligations of citizenship.

Some naturalization examiners are considerate people who seem genuinely to like to grant applications, if at all possible, rather than to deny them. And the I.N.S., as a matter of policy, is urging legal residents to become naturalized citizens. You might get lucky.

38. *I am fifteen years old, and have had my green card for five years. My parents* *have had their green cards for that long, but do not plan to file for naturalization. Can I go ahead and file for naturalization on my own?*

No. Not right now. If your parents became citizens, you could file for naturalization now. But, as it is, you will have to wait until you turn eighteen before being able for file on your own.

Appendix

1. *How to Keep up With New Developments in the Law*

Immigration law changes rapidly, and sometimes in surprising ways. A new statute, or I.N.S. rule, may make your situation much easier, or much more difficult. Your lawyer, if you have one, will tell you how new developments affect your situation. But it is also possible for you to do some studying and keep up with the law on your own. We have several suggestions.

Weekly Newspapers with Immigration Updates—There are undoubtedly more than two, but, for the time being, we recommend two weekly newspapers that contain columns on new developments in the immigration law and I.N.S. rules. One is aimed at foreign citizens of Irish background, the other at foreign citizens of Indian background. But they are useful to foreign citizens of any national background, and, indeed, to U.S. citizens. They are:

- *India Abroad.* Subscription address: 43 West 24TH Street, New York, NY 10011. Tel. (212) 645-2369. Annual subscription is $30. The weekly article on immigration is written by Allen E. Kaye, Esq.

- *The Irish Voice.* Subscription address: 432 Park Avenue South, New York, NY 10016. Tel. (212) 684-3366. Annual subscription is $30. The weekly column with answers to readers' questions is written by Debbie McGoldrick, Esq.

Monthly Magazine with Immigration Updates—In addition to these weekly newspapers, there is a reasonably priced monthly magazine that is useful for updates on new developments in the law. It is:
- *U.S. Immigrant.* P.O. Box 257, Woodland Hills, CA 91365-0257. An annual subscription is $34.95. The publication includes photocopies of I.N.S. Forms discussed in the articles, but does not include the I.N.S. instructions to the forms.

You should be able to find *India Abroad* and *The Irish Voice* at many public libraries. The *U.S. Immigrant* monthly may also be in your public library. If these publications are not in your library, speak to the librarian and suggest that the library subscribe to them.

2. *How to Find a Good Immigration Lawyer*

Annual Directory of Immigration Lawyers—The American Immigration Lawyers Association (AILA), 1400 I Street, NW, Suite 1200, Washington DC 20005, Tel. (202) 371-9377.

This leading national organization of immigration lawyers publishes an annual directory that lists the names, addresses, and phone and fax numbers of the immigration lawyers who are members of the organization. This information, at the present time, is not available to the general public, and AILA does not make referrals.

However, you might keep this in mind: immigration lawyers who are members of AILA have the reputation as being well informed and ethical. It is fair to assume that you will not be misled, or "ripped off," by a member of AILA. As you make inquiry, and "shop" for an immigration lawyer of your choice, you would be well advised to ask him or her if they are members of AILA. If they are, they have probably done their homework, and are up on the latest developments in the law.

Many immigration lawyers advertise in weekly newspapers that are aimed at particular nationality groups. Depending upon your national background, you may wish to pick up such a newspaper at the newsstand, or look it up in a library, and make up your own list of immigration lawyers. Many lawyers (not all) will give you an initial consultation free of charge. That first meeting will also give you an impression of whether you and this particular lawyer will work well together, and whether his or her fees are in the range that you can manage. Again, you might ask them if they are members of AILA.

You should also use the phone book. Look under Bar Association, and make some phone calls. Ask whether the state or city association has a list of immigration lawyers near where you live or work. You can also ask whether there are pro bono (no fee) lawyers who they can recommend to handle immigration matters. When you contact a lawyer, you might ask if he or she is a member of AILA.

State by State Listing of Free or Low-Cost Immigration Counseling Organizations—The National Immigration Law Center of Los Angeles, California publishes an extensive list of names, telephone and fax numbers of nonprofit agencies that assist in immigration matters. This extensive and extremely useful list may be obtained, for a fee of $5.00, by writing to: National Immigration Law Center of Los Angeles, 1102 S. Crenshaw Blvd., Los Angeles, California 90019. A version of the list is also reproduced in the work entitled *How to Get a Green Card*, by Loida Nicholas Lewis, Esq., Nolo Press, Berkeley, California.

Index

The first number is the chapter, the numbers following refer to the questions in that chapter. For example: 5: 4-6 means chapter 5, Questions 4 to 6.

ALLWORTH BOOKS

Allworth Press publishes quality books to help individuals and small businesses. Titles include:

Your Living Trust and Estate Plan by Harvey J. Platt
(softcover, 6 × 9, 224 pages, $14.95)

Smart Maneuvers: Taking Control of Your Career and Personal Success in the Information Age by Carl W. Battle
(softcover, 6 × 9, 224 pages, $12.95)

Retire Smart by David and Virginia Cleary
(softcover, 6 × 9, 224 pages, $12.95)

Senior Counsel: Legal and Financial Strategies for Age 50 and Beyond by Carl W. Battle
(softcover, 6¾ × 10, 256 pages, $16.95)

The Unemployment Survival Handbook by Nina Schuyler
(softcover, 6 × 9, 144 pages, $9.95)

The Family Legal Companion by Thomas Hauser
(softcover, 6 × 9, 256 pages, $16.95)

Hers: The Wise Woman's Guide to Starting a Business on $2,000 or Less by Carol Milano
(softcover, 6 × 9, 208 pages, $12.95)

Legal-Wise: Self-Help Legal Forms for Everyone, Second Edition by Carl W. Battle
(softcover, 8½ × 11, 208 pages, $16.95)

Legal Guide for the Visual Artist, Third Edition by Tad Crawford
(softcover, 8½ × 11, 256 pages, $19.95)

Wedding Photography and Video by Chuck Delaney
(softcover, 6 × 9, 160 pages, $10.95)

Travel Photography by Susan McCartney
(softcover, 6¾ × 10, 384 pages, 20 illustrations, $22.95)

Nature and Wildlife Photography by Susan McCartney
(softcover, 6¾ × 10, 256 pages, 15 B+W photographs, $18.95)

On Becoming an Artist by Daniel Grant

(softcover, 6 × 9, 192 pages, $12.95)

Please write to request our free catalog. If you wish to order a book, send your check or money order to Allworth Press, 10 East 23RD Street, Suite 400, New York, NY 10010. Include $5 for shipping and handling for the first book ordered and $1 for each additional book. Ten dollars plus $1 for each additional book if ordering from Canada. New York State residents must add sales tax.

If you wish to see our catalog on the World Wide Web, you can find us at Millenium Productions' Art and Technology Web site:

http://www.arts-online.com/allworth/home.html

or at

http://interport.net/~allworth